Contents

Preface

Delphi is a sophisticated Windows programming environment, suitable for beginners and professional programmers alike. The application lets you create self-contained, user-friendly Windows applications in a very short time. Your program's windows are 'drawn' on the screen, so that you can always see exactly what the eventual application will look like. This design work is done without writing any code, bypassing the more traditional, trial-and-error approach of pre-Windows programming languages.

When the user interface is complete, there is still a great deal of work to be done, of course. However, the Delphi programming language is both powerful and easy to master, so even complex tasks can be finished surprisingly quickly.

Delphi 3 has been designed specifically for the 32-bit environments of Windows 95 and Windows NT. In order to create 16-bit programs for Windows 3.1 you must use the earlier version, Delphi 1 (which is supplied with the latest version). There is little difference in the two versions of the programming language, so most of the instructions and programs in this book can be applied equally to both versions of the product.

This book is aimed at those who are new to programming, or new to Delphi. No previous programming experience is necessary, though familiarity with the use of Windows is assumed.

Delphi is a comprehensive programming environment and a book of this size can only give a brief introduction to the subject. However, the information given here should be enough to give you a flavour of Delphi and show you its potential for developing professional Windows applications.

Acknowledgements

I would like to thank Borland International for their assistance while this book was in preparation.

1 Overview

Starting Delphi

Delphi is a powerful Windows development tool, which allows you to produce self-contained Windows applications quickly and effectively. Delphi contains a visual development environment that generates the necessary code for the user interface. You can modify this code or add new procedures that will extend the effects of the user's actions. All code is developed using the Pascal programming language, which has been extended to handle the additional requirements of Windows applications.

Delphi editions

The latest version of Delphi comes in three different editions:

● Delphi Standard – creates fully-functional Windows applications using a set of standard tools

● Delphi Professional – adds the tools necessary to create distributable applications for all PC environments

● Delphi Client/Server – includes facilities for setting up client/server applications

This book concentrates on the Delphi Standard features, which are common to all three editions.

Windows versions

Delphi 3 is supplied only as a 32-bit version and must therefore be run under either Windows 95 or Windows NT (version 3.51 or later). Applications created with Delphi 3 can be run only under Windows 95 or Windows NT.

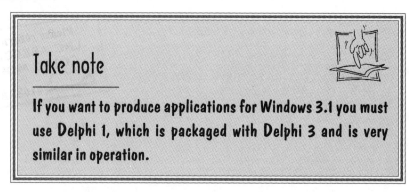

Take note

If you want to produce applications for Windows 3.1 you must use Delphi 1, which is packaged with Delphi 3 and is very similar in operation.

Installation

Delphi is installed in a similar way to most other Windows applications.

Take note

If you want to develop Windows 3.1 applications, click on the Delphi 1 icon.

1   Load the Delphi CD. The installation program will run automatically.

2   Click on Delphi 3 Professional and follow the instructions as they appear on screen.

At the end of the set-up process, the installation program will add an option to the Programs menu, leading to the main Delphi 3 program plus some subsidiary programs.

Tip

If you are short of hard disk space you do not have to install the whole application (which requires about 130Mb); instead, select the Custom installation and choose only the features you need. For instance, you may omit the database tools or the sample programs. The missing parts can be added later by re-running the installation program.

Delphi folder

Tip

For Windows 95, you can create a Delphi folder and shortcut icon. In Explorer, open the Windows | Start Menu | Programs folder and copy the Borland Delphi folder icon to the Windows | Desktop folder (click on the Delphi folder, hold down [Ctrl] and drag the folder onto 'Desktop').

Running Delphi

The installation process will have created a number of menu options and icons, one of which can be used to run the application.

Starting the program

1 Minimise any other applications that are currently running and minimise any folders.

2 Click on the Start button, then on Programs, Borland Delphi 3 and, finally, on Delphi 3.

Alternatively, if you have created a Delphi folder, click on the Delphi 3 icon.

Delphi folder

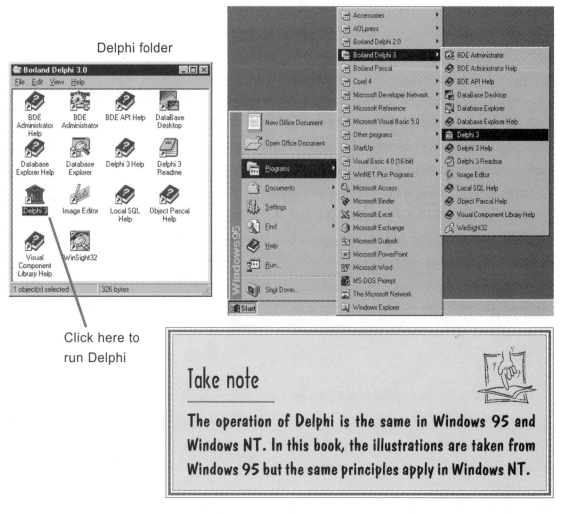

Click here to run Delphi

Take note

The operation of Delphi is the same in Windows 95 and Windows NT. In this book, the illustrations are taken from Windows 95 but the same principles apply in Windows NT.

The Delphi display

The Delphi display is confusing when you first see it. Unlike most other Windows applications, Delphi comprises a number of separate windows. Initially, four of these windows will be open; others will pop up as you develop your application.

Object Inspector – sets the appearance and behaviour of windows and other objects

Main window – select actions from menus or toolbar and choose components for your application

Form 1 – the first window for your application

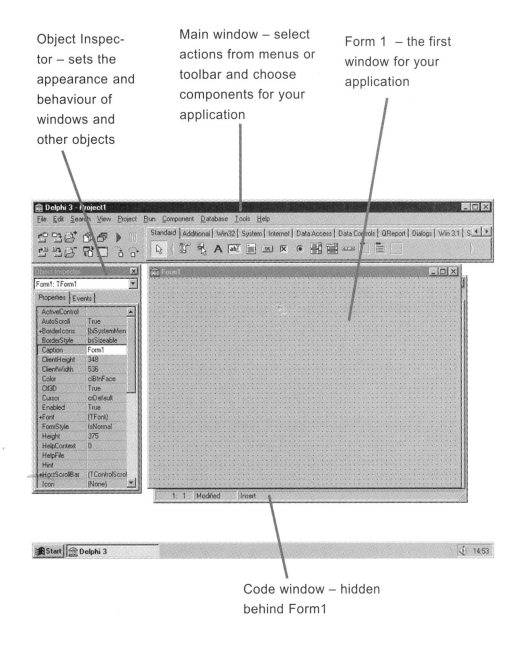

Code window – hidden behind Form1

Delphi windows

Delphi consists of a main window and a number of subsidiary windows. It is well worth familiarising yourself with the most important windows before you start creating an application.

Main window

The **main window** contains all the elements you would expect to find in a Windows application:

- The **title bar** contains the name of your current project (initially Project1) and the usual buttons for minimising, maximising and closing the window.

- The **menu bar** includes nine pop-down menus. Many of the options in these menus are described later in the book.

- The **speedbar** contains a number of icons that provide shortcuts to the most frequently used Delphi operations, such as saving a file or running the application.

In addition to these standard Windows elements, there is a **component palette**, which is used for building up the visible elements of your application.

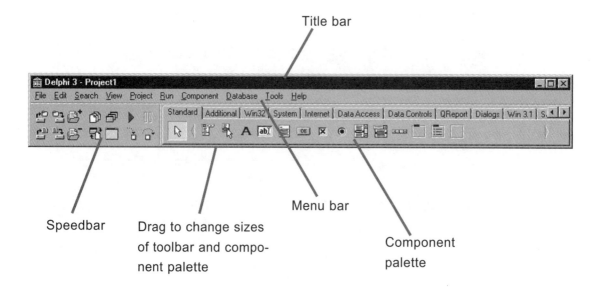

Title bar

Speedbar

Drag to change sizes
of toolbar and compo-
nent palette

Menu bar

Component
palette

Component palette

Any window contains a number of different objects: command buttons, text boxes, labels and so on. These are called **components**. When you are creating a window for a Delphi application, these components are added by dragging them from the **component palette**.

There are a large number of components available to you when you start your application – and you can add more components later (either from a third-party supplier or ones you have created yourself). The components are grouped together according to the function they perform; by clicking on one of the tabs along the top of the palette you can display another group of components. More tabs can be shown by clicking on the arrow buttons on the right-hand side.

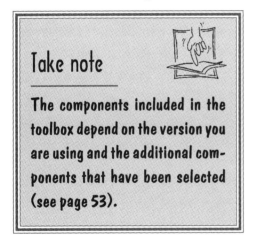

Take note

The components included in the toolbox depend on the version you are using and the additional components that have been selected (see page 53).

For large groups of components (or if you have reduced the width of the palette), you can scroll through the components by clicking on the arrows at either end of the palette.

The pointer icon on the left of the palette is used for selecting existing components on a window so that they can be moved, resized or changed in some other way.

The components are described in detail in Chapter 3.

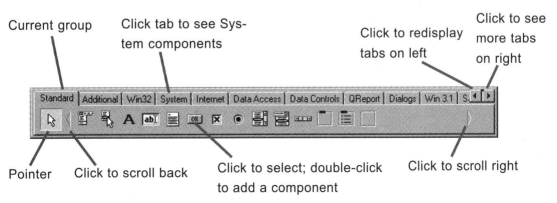

Current group | Click tab to see System components | Click to redisplay tabs on left | Click to see more tabs on right

Pointer | Click to scroll back | Click to select; double-click to add a component | Click to scroll right

Form1 window

A Delphi application usually consists of one or more windows. At the design stage, these windows are called **forms**. To start you off, Delphi supplies a single form, called Form1. This form will be renamed and resized when you begin to develop the application; other forms will be added as required.

As you add new forms, the display will become even more cluttered. However, you can hide, or minimise windows when you don't need them – see page 10.

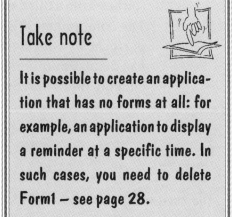

Take note

It is possible to create an application that has no forms at all: for example, an application to display a reminder at a specific time. In such cases, you need to delete Form1 – see page 28.

Code window

Clicking on the edges of the window just behind Form1 brings the **code window** to the top. This is where the code that drives the

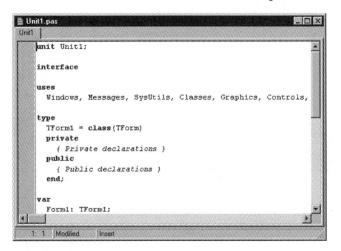

application is created. Delphi starts off by giving you the skeleton of a program, and it will add more code as you develop the visual part of the application. Later, you will expand the capabilities of the application by inserting your own code (see Chapter 4).

Object Inspector

Each form, and each component on a form, has a set of **properties**. These determine the appearance of the form or component and the way in which it behaves. A form has properties that specify how big it is and where it is on the screen, whether it is visible when the application starts, whether it has Minimise and Maximise buttons and so on. Most components have a large number of properties, some of which are similar to those of forms, others that are unique to the component. Each type of component has a different set of properties.

In addition, each form or component can respond to a number of **events**: for example, being clicked or dragged.

The Object Inspector window displays the properties and events for the selected form or component, and allows you to change the properties or select the response to each event. Some of the more important properties are described in Chapters 2 and 3. Events are described in Chapter 4.

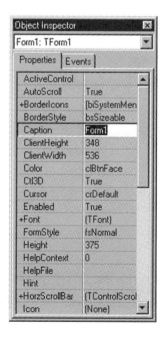

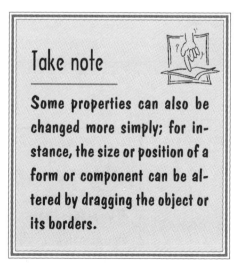

Take note

Some properties can also be changed more simply; for instance, the size or position of a form or component can be altered by dragging the object or its borders.

View options

The Object Inspector window can be cleared from the screen by clicking on the Close button in the top right-hand corner of the window. The application windows (Form1 and the code window) can be moved out of the way by clicking on their Minimise buttons.

To redisplay the Object Inspector window, click on the appropriate option in the View menu or press function key **[F11]**; to redisplay Form1 and the code window, click on their Minimise or Maximise buttons.

The windows can also be moved by dragging the title bar or resized by dragging their corners or edges. The Maximise button on Form1 expands the window to fill the whole screen; the code window's Maximise button expands the window to fill the remaining space below the main window.

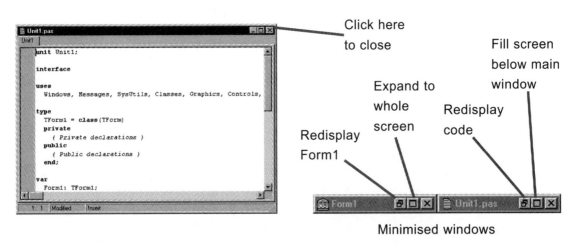

Click here to close

Fill screen below main window

Expand to whole screen

Redisplay code

Redisplay Form1

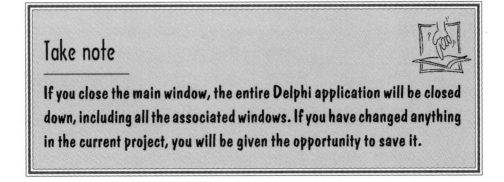

Minimised windows

Take note

If you close the main window, the entire Delphi application will be closed down, including all the associated windows. If you have changed anything in the current project, you will be given the opportunity to save it.

Getting help

Delphi is supplied with extensive documentation, which provides a detailed explanation of many aspects of program development. The printed manuals include:

- The *User's Guide*, which provides an introduction to Delphi

- The *Visual Component Library Reference* (2 volumes), which describes each component in detail

- The *Object Pascal Language Guide*, which gives a complete reference to the Delphi programming language

- The *Developer's Guide*, which covers advanced topics (such as creating your own components, database applications and access to the Internet)

As well as the printed manuals, Delphi holds a great deal of information in the form of on-line help. Although this can be tricky to use, it is worth learning how to extract information, as some topics are covered only in on-line help and do not appear in the printed documentation.

Click here for Contents list

Click here for index

Search for particular words or phrases, anywhere in Help

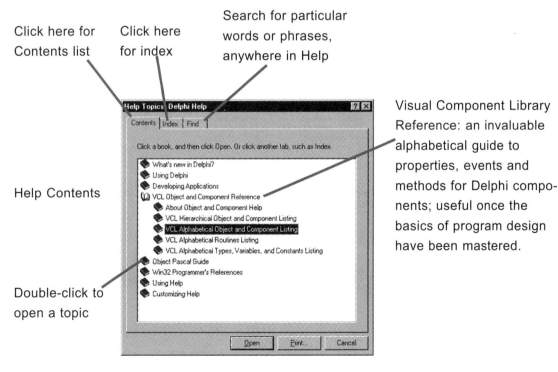

Help Contents

Double-click to open a topic

Visual Component Library Reference: an invaluable alphabetical guide to properties, events and methods for Delphi components; useful once the basics of program design have been mastered.

Help options

You can get on-line help in a number of ways:

● Click on Help in the menu bar at the top of the main window and then on Contents in the drop-down menu. This leads to the Help Contents window, where a number of topics are displayed (including on-line versions of the manuals). Double-clicking on a topic eventually takes you to the relevant help screen.

● Click on the Index tab in the Help window to display the Index list (or select Keyword Search from the Help menu). The main part of this window lists the topics available in on-line help; you can either scroll through the list or start typing in the text box at the top to go straight to an item in the index. Double-click on an index item; this will either show the corresponding help or list relevant topics.

Type text to find
index entry

Double-click on
an item to show
related topics

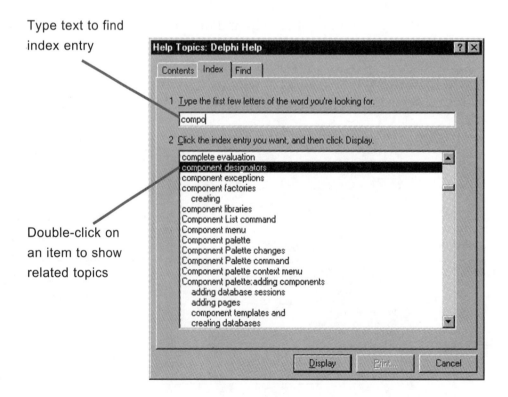

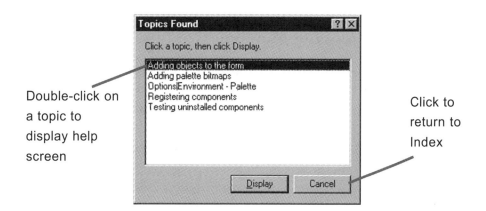

Double-click on
a topic to
display help
screen

Click to
return to
Index

- Press function key **[F1]** (context-sensitive help) to go straight to the topic relating to your current activity. For instance, if you click on the Object Inspector and press **[F1]** you will get information on the property or event that is highlighted; pressing **[F1]** on an item in the component palette gives you a description of the component. You can also get context-sensitive help on specific parts of a form, error messages and individual keywords when writing code.

When you have finished with the help screen, remove it by clicking on the Close button.

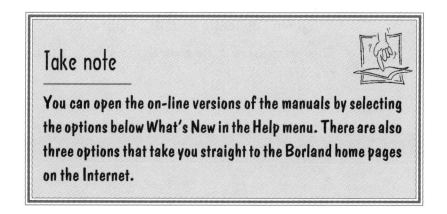

Take note

You can open the on-line versions of the manuals by selecting the options below What's New in the Help menu. There are also three options that take you straight to the Borland home pages on the Internet.

Leaving Delphi

You can get out of Delphi at any time, either temporarily (while you work on some other application) or permanently.

Suspending Delphi

To suspend Delphi temporarily, click on the Minimise button on the main window and then start another application.

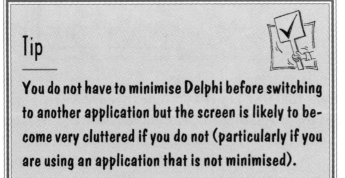

Tip

You do not have to minimise Delphi before switching to another application but the screen is likely to become very cluttered if you do not (particularly if you are using an application that is not minimised).

To get back into Delphi, use one of these methods:

● If Delphi was minimised, click on the taskbar button.

● If any part of any Delphi window is visible, click on it.

● Press **[Alt-Esc]** or **[Alt-Tab]** repeatedly to cycle through the open applications until Delphi is active.

The program will be exactly as you left it and all windows will be restored.

Exiting Delphi

To close down Delphi altogether, select File I Exit. Alternatively, click on the Close button. If you have made any changes to the current project you are asked if you want to save them.

- Click on Yes (or press **[Enter]**) to save the changes. (If this is the first time the project has been saved, a filename will be needed – see page 29.)

- Click on No to abandon the changes – no further confirmation is requested.

- Click on Cancel (or press **[Esc]**) to continue working in Delphi.

If you attempt to close down the computer without ending Delphi, Windows will close Delphi for you and the same options will be given for any unsaved projects.

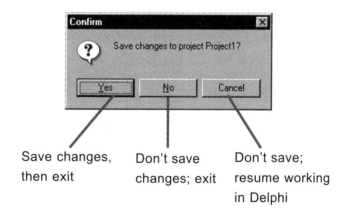

Save changes,   Don't save   Don't save;
then exit   changes; exit   resume working
                                    in Delphi

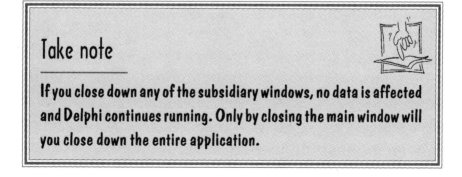

Take note

If you close down any of the subsidiary windows, no data is affected and Delphi continues running. Only by closing the main window will you close down the entire application.

Exercises

1   Start Delphi and identify the windows that are displayed.

2   Close individual windows and then re-open them again. Move the windows to more convenient positions; resize them where appropriate. Close or minimise all subsidiary windows, then restore them.

3   Search for help relating to the Object Inspector window.

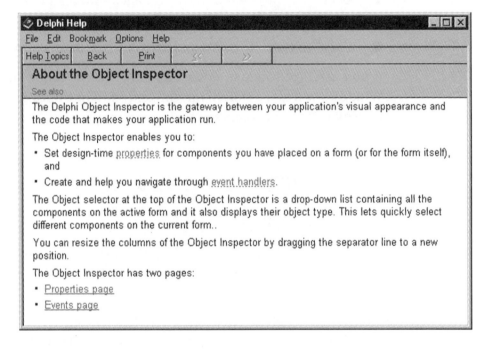

4   Minimise the main Delphi application and then re-activate it.

5   Exit Delphi.

For solutions to these exercises, see page 178.

2 Forms

The first form

Any Windows 95 application is made up of one or more distinct **windows**. A window can be used to display information, to allow the user to enter data or to provide options for the user to select.

As we have seen, Delphi has several windows: the main window, Object Inspector, Form1, code window and others (which will be displayed as they are needed). The main window provides options for you to select; the Object Inspector window provides a description of a particular object and lets you make changes; the Form1 window will become the first window for your application; and the code window lets you view and change the programming code behind your application.

At the development stage, the windows that make up a finished Delphi application are called **forms**. The forms you create become the windows through which the user accesses your application. This is the **user interface** (UI).

Not all of the windows need be visible when the user starts up the application; in most applications, only a single 'front-end' window is displayed when the application is run, other windows appearing as they are needed.

It is up to you, when designing a form, to decide how the window will behave: whether it is on-screen initially; whether the user can minimise or resize it; and so on. However, you should remember that once a window has been displayed it is the user who decides the order in which things happen and when the window will be closed down. The more objects (buttons, scroll bars, text boxes etc.) you put on a form, the less control you have over the user's actions.

A form starts off as an empty window, which may have a title bar and control buttons (Control-menu box, Minimise button, Maximise button, Close button). Within it, you may add other objects: buttons, lists, check boxes etc.

Form files

The details of each form are stored in a separate **form file**, with a DFM extension. This holds information such as the initial size of the form, its position, the title text and so on.

There will be some code attached to the form, determining how the application will respond when the user takes action on the window's controls. For instance, when the user closes the window, the code attached to the form should take any necessary action on data that has been entered and then remove the window. All the code that is specific to a particular form is stored in a separate Pascal file, with the same filename as the form file but an extension of PAS.

All these files go together to make up the project from which the application is built. The Project Manager window lists the project files. You can add existing files to a project or remove files. A file can be part of more than one project; for example, you may use the same window in two independent applications. Removing a file from a project does not affect the file itself; it is still intact on disk. The Project Manager is displayed by selecting the appropriate option from the View menu.

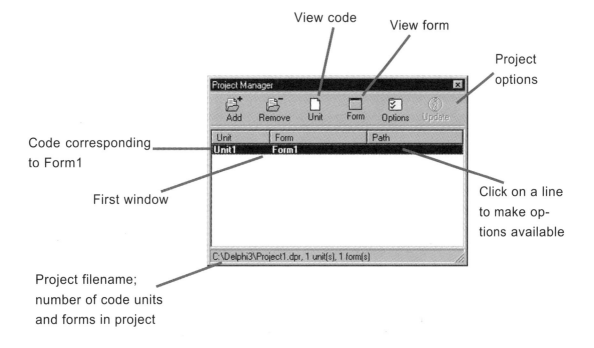

View code

View form

Project
options

Code corresponding
to Form1

First window

Click on a line
to make op-
tions available

Project filename;
number of code units
and forms in project

Form1

Delphi supplies a default form to start the project: Form1. You can use this as your application's front-end window. The form can be customised as follows:

1. Increase or decrease the size of the window by dragging one of the form's corners or its borders.

2. Move the form to a suitable position by dragging the Form1 title bar; this will be the window's initial position when the program is run.

Other changes to the window and the way in which it behaves are made by altering the form's properties.

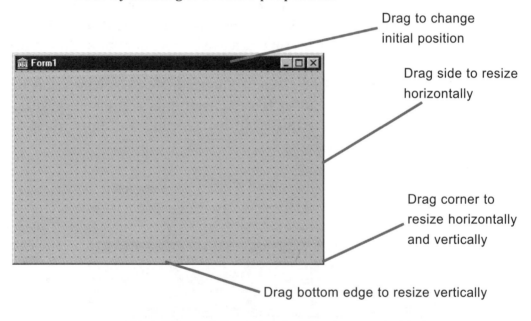

Drag to change initial position

Drag side to resize horizontally

Drag corner to resize horizontally and vertically

Drag bottom edge to resize vertically

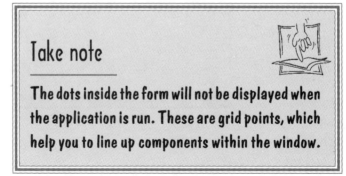

Take note

The dots inside the form will not be displayed when the application is run. These are grid points, which help you to line up components within the window.

Form properties

The appearance and behaviour of a window are determined by the corresponding form's **properties**. These specify such details as the size and position of the window, whether it can be minimised or closed, and so on. For each property, there is a single **setting**.

When you click on Form1, the properties are listed in the Object Inspector window, in the left-hand column. The corresponding settings are shown on the right. Any property can be changed by clicking on the appropriate line. In some cases, there are a fixed number of options and you must choose from a drop-down list; for others, a value for the setting can be typed in directly. Some property items (with a '+' to the left) represent a group of properties.

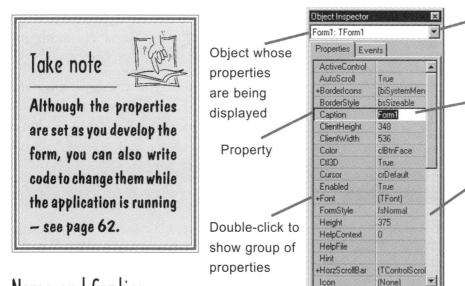

Take note

Although the properties are set as you develop the form, you can also write code to change them while the application is running – see page 62.

Object whose properties are being displayed

Property

Double-click to show group of properties

Click to list properties

Setting

Click to show more properties

Name and Caption

The **Name** of the form is the name that appears in the Project Manager window; the **Caption** is the piece of text that appears in the title bar (for the front-end window, usually the application title). Either can be changed by clicking on the existing setting and retyping it.

The Name property should be changed to something that will tell you what the form does. The Name will be used in the creation of the filename, so should be kept short: for example, 'MainForm' for the front-end window. After changing the Name, change the Caption (which will have defaulted to the new Name).

The border style

The **BorderStyle** property specifies the type of border and elements that may appear in the title area. The most useful options are:

bsDialog The window is a dialogue box. It may have a title bar and Control-menu button but cannot have the other control buttons. It cannot be resized by the user.

bsNone There is no border; the window has no title bar or control buttons – useful for message boxes.

bsSingle The window may have a title bar, Control-menu box, Close button, Minimise button and Maximise button. The user cannot change the window size by dragging the border. This style is used for windows with a fixed number of components (e.g. data entry forms).

bsSizeable The window may have any of the bsSingle controls and may also be resized by the user. This is the default for all new forms and is used anywhere that the user may need to resize the form (e.g. text windows, spreadsheets, pictures).

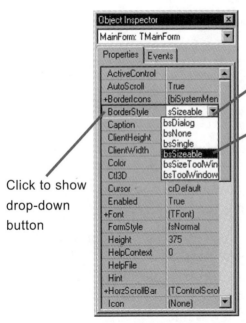

Click to show drop-down button

Click to display list of options

Click to select an option

Two other options, bsToolWindow and bsSizeToolWin, are used in the creation of speedbars.

To select a border option, click on BorderStyle. A down-arrow button appears on the right. Click on this, and a drop-down list is displayed. Click on one of the options in the list to change the setting.

Title bar and buttons

If BorderStyle is bsNone, the window will have no title bar and therefore no buttons. For any other setting a title bar is displayed and may include the usual Windows buttons. The inclusion of a Control-menu box, Minimise button and Maximise button are determined by the settings of the **biSystemMenu**, **biMinimize** and **biMaximize** properties respectively. These are part of the BorderIcons group and are displayed by double-clicking on the property name.

There is also a **biHelp** property, which is effective if the style is bsDialog or if the Minimise and Maximise buttons are omitted. This property adds a ? button, which can be used for providing help on any aspect of the window.

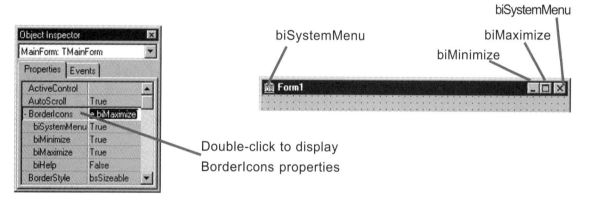

Double-click to display
BorderIcons properties

Each of these properties has two possible settings: True or False. The True setting indicates that the button is included (and therefore that the user may click on it); False means that the button will not be available.

The Close button is included only when there is a Control-menu box.

Position and size

The size of a form can be altered by dragging its borders; its position can be modified by dragging the title bar. When you do so, you change the following properties:

Left   Distance of left border from left-hand edge of screen

Top   Distance of top border from top of screen

23

Width   Width of form (including borders)

Height   Height of form (including borders and title bar)

For precise form size and position, these settings can be entered directly in the Properties window. Entering the settings manually also ensures consistency between windows.

All sizes are measured in pixels. For high-resolution screens (with more pixels across and down the screen), text appears much smaller and more can be fitted on the screen; in a similar way, windows will appear smaller and take up less space on a high-resolution screen.

Tip

When developing on a high-resolution screen, remember that end users may have screens of lower resolution. Either make sure that windows will have an initial position towards the left and top of the screen, or use the screen dimensions to calculate the position and size at run time – see **Chapter 4.**

Visible and Enabled

A window should be displayed only when it is needed; this is controlled by the form's Visible property. When Visible is True, the window appears on the screen in its predefined position; when Visible is False, the window is hidden. Usually, the front-end form is visible and all other forms are initially hidden.

Only one window can be **active** at a time; the colour of the title bar is used by Windows to show which window is active. Clicking on a window makes it active (and deactivates all other windows). Even though a form is visible, you may not want the user to be able to access it. For instance, when a dialogue box is displayed, you may not want the user to click on the window behind it until the dialogue is closed. When the Enabled property for a form is True, users can click on the window to make it active; when the property is False, clicking on the window has no effect.

Saving the form

Like all other computer applications, you should save your work regularly. It can take a long time to set up a form just as you want it and it takes only a few seconds to save it.

Creating a directory

Start by creating a new directory for the application. You will usually end up with a large number of files for any project and these are much easier to handle if they are stored away together in their own directory.

Take note

To create a directory, use File | New | Folder in the Windows 95 Explorer. Alternatively, you can create a directory when you first save the file.

The form and code files

As described above, the details of the form are saved in a form file. This file holds everything that is needed to construct the form: its properties, its components and their properties. The form's code is held in a corresponding Pascal file. The files are saved together.

Take note

The saved form can be used in any number of projects. This provides consistency between your applications and reduces the amount of development that has to be done.

Tip

In future, you can quickly save the current form by pressing [Ctrl-S]. Do this every few minutes.

Saving the file

To save the current form and its code, select File | Save As from the Delphi menu bar, change to the new directory, and give the file a suitable name. Delphi will suggest a filename of Unit1.pas. Type a new name (e.g. MainUnit). Delphi will add a PAS extension. The corresponding form file will be saved as MainUnit.dfm. The name you give must be different to the Name property for the form (i.e. you cannot use MainForm.pas).

After saving the file, the filename you specified appears in the Project Manager window, to the left of the Name.

Select directory

Create new directory

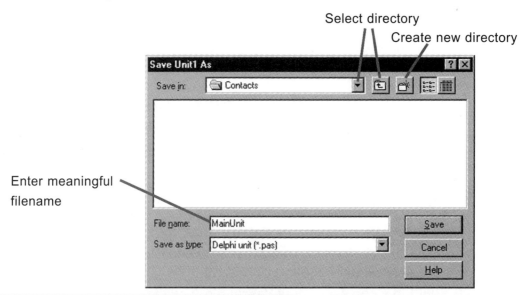

Enter meaningful filename

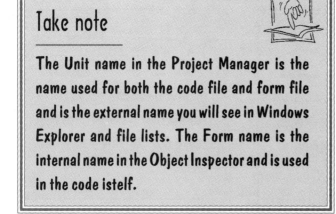

Take note

The Unit name in the Project Manager is the name used for both the code file and form file and is the external name you will see in Windows Explorer and file lists. The Form name is the internal name in the Object Inspector and is used in the code istelf.

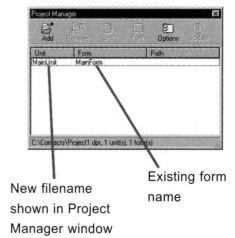

New filename shown in Project Manager window

Existing form name

Adding new forms

Most applications need a number of windows, and the forms for these can be created in much the same way as the first form. To add a new form, select File | New Form from the Delphi menu (or click on the New Form button on the speedbar). A blank form is displayed, with the same default settings as the original Form1. An entry for this form will be added to the Project Manager window. The property settings can be changed by double-clicking on the form name in the Project Manager and then changing values in the Object Inspector window.

The following table lists suitable property settings for three different types of form (with dimensions suitable for an 800x600 screen):

Property	Data Entry Window	Text Entry Window	Message Box
Name	DataForm	TextForm	Mess1Form
Filename	DataUnit.pas	TextUnit.pas	Mes1Unit.pas
Caption	Data Entry	Text Entry	Error
Left	280	80	200
Top	80	240	200
Width	400	440	320
Height	350	300	100
BorderStyle	bsSingle	bsSizeable	bsDialog
biSystemMenu	True	True	False
biMinimize	True	True	False
biMaximize	False	True	False

Each form should be saved with File | Save As. This option saves the **current** form, so make sure you have clicked on the form you want to save. Keep all forms for the project in the same directory.

After making further changes to a form, the file should be saved with File | Save (or click on the form and press **[Ctrl-S]**).

Adding existing forms

Existing form files can be added to the project at any time. Click on the Add button in the Project Manager (or click on Add File To Project in the speedbar or select Project | Add To Project). Then choose the unit (.PAS) file from the file list. In this way, you can restore forms that were previously removed. You can also add in forms that were created for other projects.

Add file
to project

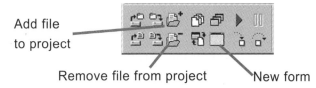

Removing forms

Remove file from project   New form

If a form is no longer needed, it can be removed from the project. On the Project Manager window, click on the form name and then on the Remove button (or use the Remove File From Project button on the speedbar or the Project | Remove From Project option).

Although the form is removed from the project, the form and code files themselves are unaffected and can be restored later if required.

Add file
to project

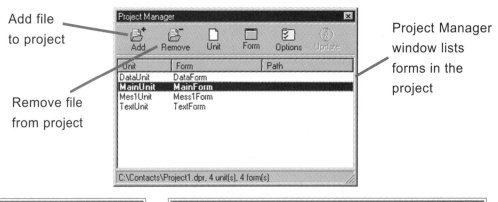

Remove file
from project

Project Manager
window lists
forms in the
project

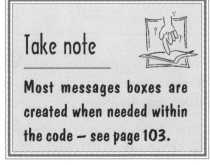

Take note

Most messages boxes are created when needed within the code – see page 103.

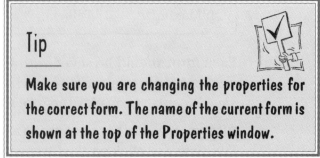

Tip

Make sure you are changing the properties for the correct form. The name of the current form is shown at the top of the Properties window.

Saving and running

Usually, an application is made up of several windows, each of which is created from a form in a DFM file with code in a corresponding PAS file. The application as a whole has a **project file**, which defines the forms, programs and other files that go together to make up the finished project.

The current project can be saved with File|Save Project As. Again, save it in the project directory with a name that identifies the project as a whole. The name must be different to all of the other names you have used so far. The file is given a DPR extension. If any form has changed, it will be saved at the same time.

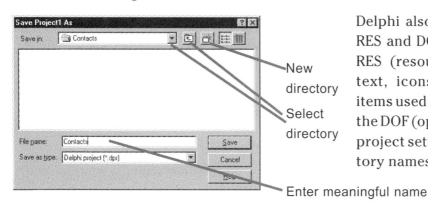

New directory

Select directory

Enter meaningful name

Delphi also creates files with RES and DOF extensions. The RES (resource) file contains text, icons and other fixed items used in your application; the DOF (options) file contains project settings, such as directory names.

Running the application

To test the program, select Run from the Run menu (or press **[F9]**). The first window should pop up straight away. It may not appear very impressive but all the buttons on the window should behave as you would expect. The Minimise and Maximise buttons (if included) will reduce the application to an icon or blow it up to full-screen size, respectively. The window can be moved or resized (depending on the setting for BorderStyle). Any other windows will not be visible yet – you need to add some program code before they can be seen.

Finally, you can close the application by clicking on the Close button in the top right-hand corner of the window.

When you run the application, Delphi creates a file with an EXE extension for the project and a DCU (compiled unit) file for each form.

Exercises

The exercises in this book will build up an application for storing details of individuals (for example, a company's customers) and contacts with those individuals. This application can be modified to suit many other purposes (such as a membership database or a program to store records of correspondence).

1   Create a new directory.

2   Create a front-end form, with a Minimise button but no Maximise button. The form should be of fixed size, with a suitable title. Name it 'MainForm' and save it in a file called MainUnit.dfm (with code in MainUnit.pas).

3   Create a form for entering data, again with no Maximise button and of fixed size. Name it 'DetailsForm' and save it with a suitable filename.

4   Create a form for entering text. This form should be sizable. Name it 'CallsForm' and save it with a suitable filename.

5   Save the project with the filename Contacts.dpr.

6   Run the application to check that the front-end window is displayed correctly. Save any changes.

For solutions to these exercises, see page 178.

3 Components

Adding components

All windows have one or more **components**. These are objects that display information or allow the user to perform an action: for instance, command buttons, text boxes, option buttons and scroll bars.

Any combination of components can be placed on a form but you should remember that when the application is run the user will be free to use the components in any order (subject to any restrictions you impose at development time).

For example, the message box that is displayed when you try to close Delphi without saving the project contains five components: three buttons (marked Yes, No and Cancel), a label (containing the text of the message) and an image component (containing the icon). The program forces you to click on one of the buttons but it's up to you which you choose. The action taken by the program depends on which button is clicked.

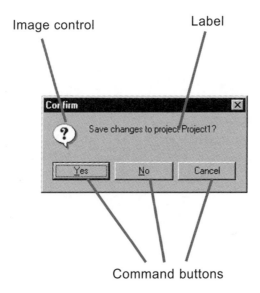

Image control   Label

Command buttons

The component palette

Delphi supplies a number of standard components for use on forms. These are represented by icons in the **component palette**. Components can be added to a form in one of two ways:

● Click on the component in the palette, then drag the pointer over the area of the form to be covered by the component.

● Double-click on the component to create an object of default size on the form.

In either case, you can change the size and position later (see *Component properties* below). The standard components are described from page 43 onwards.

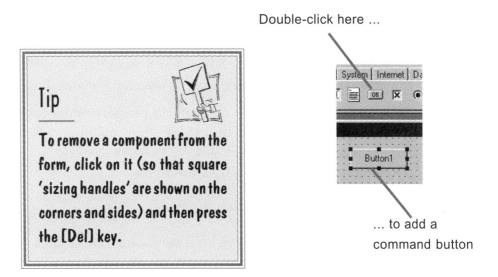

Double-click here ...

Tip

To remove a component from the form, click on it (so that square 'sizing handles' are shown on the corners and sides) and then press the [Del] key.

... to add a command button

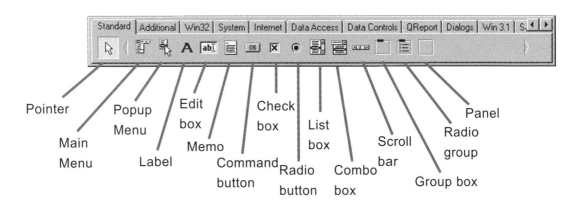

Pointer

Main Menu

Popup Menu

Label

Edit box

Memo

Command button

Check box

Radio button

List box

Combo box

Scroll bar

Group box

Panel

Radio group

Component properties

The appearance and behaviour of a component is determined by its **properties**, in the same way as for a form. The properties include not only cosmetic items – the size, colour and position of the component, for example – but also those characteristics that affect the way a component is used: the text shown on it, the user actions that are allowed etc.

The properties are different for each type of component and in each case the system provides a default. Most defaults are quite satisfactory so there are usually only a very few properties that need to be changed.

As for forms, you will set the properties when developing the project but they may also be changed while the application is running.

Some properties apply to most or all of the components – for instance, every component has a Name – and most can be revised. The most important properties are given below for the standard components.

A number of other, more advanced properties are included in most components and may be useful when an application reaches an advanced stage of development. You are unlikely to use them often but it is worth knowing they are there.

Changing properties

To change the properties for a component, first click on the component so that it is selected. Small square 'handles' will appear at each corner and in the middle of each side. The Object Inspector window will show the name of the control at the top (initially a default name, consisting of the control type and a number); you will see the properties that are listed change each time you select a different type of component.

Remember that all components of the same type will have the same properties but each component will be given different settings. For example, all command buttons have Name, Width and Caption properties; the settings for one button may be ButtonOK, 75 and OK respectively, and for another, ButtonHelp, 50 and Help.

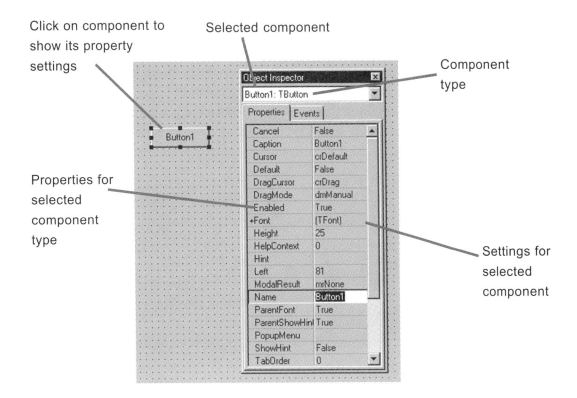

Click on component to show its property settings

Selected component

Component type

Properties for selected component type

Settings for selected component

Multiple properties

You can select a group of components in one of the following ways:

● Hold down the **[Shift]** key and then click on two or more components. Each time you click on a component, it is identified with **grey** sizing handles.

● Move the pointer to a blank area of the form and then drag it over the components. Any component that is at least partly covered by the marked rectangle is given grey sizing handles.

● A component can be removed from the group by holding down **[Shift]** and clicking on it again.

The settings can be changed for all the marked components at the same time. This method is normally used for dragging components to another part of the form but you can also make an entry in the Object Inspector window: for instance, to change the width of a group of components.

Common properties

A large number of properties are common to all or most components; these provide the basic functionality of the components. Each type of component has its own additional properties, which regulate those features that are peculiar to the component. For instance, most components can have their size and position changed but only an edit box has a PasswordChar property, which allows the box to be used for entering a password. The most useful properties are described here.

Name

Every component has a **Name**, which is used when referring to the component in a procedure (for instance, when changing the component's properties at run time). Delphi gives each new component a default name, consisting of the component type and a number: Button1, Button2, ..., Edit1, Edit2 etc. You should change these to something more meaningful. You should change the Name for all new controls, even those you think you are unlikely to use in a procedure.

The rules for names are as follows:

- Names can be up to 63 characters long.

- Names may consist of letters, numbers and underscore (_) characters; no other characters or spaces are allowed.

- Names must start with a letter or an underscore character.

- Upper and lower case letters are treated as being the same but a mixture can be used to make the name easier to identify (ButtonSaveAs is more recognisable than buttonsaveas but both refer to the same component).

- You must not use **reserved words** (such as **End** and **String**) and you should avoid **identifiers** that have a special meaning in the Pascal language (such as *Integer* and *TEdit*).

Reserved words are printed in bold type in the manuals and are displayed in bold in program code; identifiers are printed in italic type in the manuals. For a list of reserved words, search the index for 'Reserved words and standard directives'.

Caption

Most components have a **Caption**. This holds the text that appears on the surface of the component. The restrictions on the Name do not apply to the Caption; this is a purely cosmetic piece of text.

You can include an & in front of a character in the Caption to denote that character as an **accelerator key** (or **access key**). When there is an accelerator key, the component can be 'clicked' by pressing **[Alt]** and the accelerator character together. The accelerator key character is underlined in the component's caption.

It is usual to underline the first character of the Caption, unless it has already been used by another component on the same form (in which case you can select any other character in the Caption).

If two components have the same accelerator key, pressing that combination will select each one in turn. However, this should be avoided as it is confusing for users.

Edit boxes do not have a Caption; since the text typed in the box can be changed by the user, it is held in the Text property instead. The lack of a Caption means that edit boxes cannot be given an accelerator key directly. However, you can get round the problem by placing a label component next to the edit box; since a label component cannot be clicked, the accelerator key on the label acts as an accelerator key for the edit box. For the key to be effective, the **FocusControl** property of the label must be set to the edit box's Name.

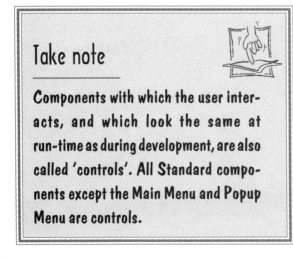

Take note

Components with which the user interacts, and which look the same at run-time as during development, are also called 'controls'. All Standard components except the Main Menu and Popup Menu are controls.

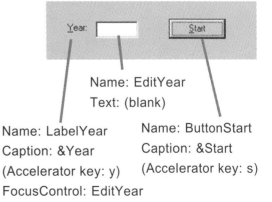

Name: EditYear
Text: (blank)

Name: LabelYear
Caption: &Year
(Accelerator key: y)
FocusControl: EditYear

Name: ButtonStart
Caption: &Start
(Accelerator key: s)

Size and position

The size and position of a component are determined by the same set of four properties as for a form: **Width** and **Height** for the size, **Left** and **Top** for position. Left and Top give the position of the top-left corner of the component relative to the top-left corner of the inside of the form.

These properties can be changed either by dragging the sizing handles on the corners and sides of the component or by entering new settings directly. Usually, dragging the sizing handles is satisfactory, as it enables you to set the size and position by eye. For precise settings, however, the properties can be adjusted manually.

By default, the same units (pixels) are used for components as for forms. When developing a form there is a background grid of points for aligning components. If you change the component size or position by dragging, the component corners 'snap' to the nearest grid points. The grid can be changed (or switched off) by choosing Tools|Environment Options and clicking on the Preferences tab; the Width and Height of the grid square can be changed and the grid snap can be turned off.

Click to turn off grid

Click to stop controls snapping to grid

Spacing of grid points (pixels)

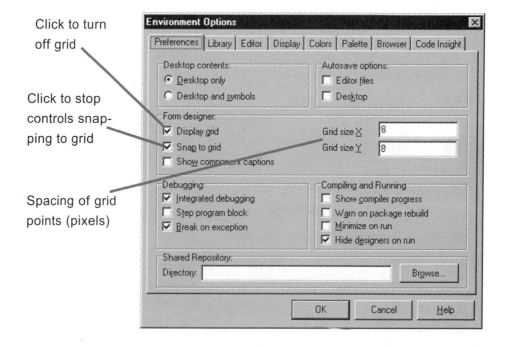

Fonts

If the component displays text, you can change the appearance with the **Font** property. When you double-click on the property, a small button appears on the right. Clicking on this displays the Font window, from which you can select the font, the style (bold, italic etc.) and the point size. You can also apply strikeout (a line through the middle of the text) and underline.

You can view or change individual font settings by double-clicking on the Font property; within the Font list, the Style property also contains an expandable list of properties.

Double-click to list Font properties

Click to display font box

Double-click to list Style properties

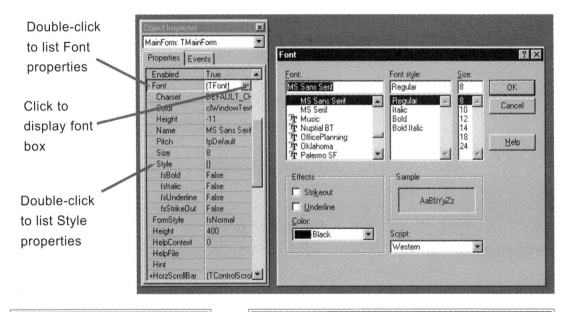

Tip

If you click on the Font list and move up and down using the arrow keys, the Sample box shows you what the text will look like.

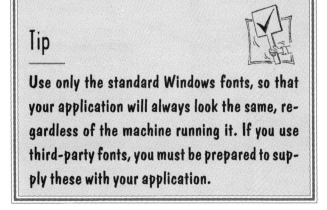

Tip

Use only the standard Windows fonts, so that your application will always look the same, regardless of the machine running it. If you use third-party fonts, you must be prepared to supply these with your application.

Colour

The component's background colour (where available) is set by the **Color** property. For components that display text, the colour of the text is determined by **Color** option in the **Font** property. The values for colours can be entered in one of three ways:

● Choosing a named colour

● Selecting from a palette

● Entering an RGB colour number

The easiest way to choose a colour is by clicking on the property. You can select from a list of standard named Windows colours (as set in the Control Panel), such as clRed or clBtnFace. Alternatively, if you double-click on the Color setting, you can choose from a colour palette. When you click on a colour square, either a numeric code or a colour name is entered in the setting box. The main disadvantage of this method is that the range of colours is limited.

You can create your own colour by entering a numeric RGB code. Each colour on the screen is made up of three elements – red, green and blue – in differing intensities. The colour is represented by a hexadecimal number in the form $00bbggrr$, where rr is the red element, gg green and bb blue. Each element can have a value between 00 (no colour) and hexadecimal FF (full intensity). The midpoint is 80.

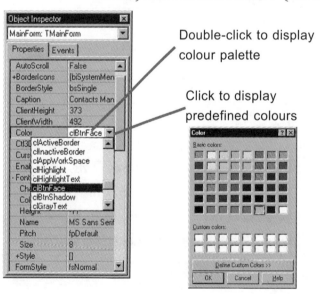

Double-click to display colour palette

Click to display predefined colours

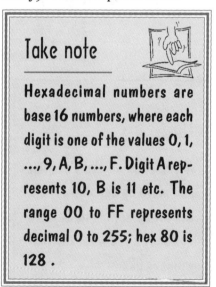

Take note

Hexadecimal numbers are base 16 numbers, where each digit is one of the values 0, 1, ..., 9, A, B, ..., F. Digit A represents 10, B is 11 etc. The range 00 to FF represents decimal 0 to 255; hex 80 is 128 .

Tab stops and focus

When the user clicks on a window, the window is said to have the **focus**; that is, it is the current window. The title bar of the window with the focus has a different colour to the others. (By default, the window with the focus has a blue title bar, the rest are grey.) Only one window can have the focus at any one time.

Similarly, one (and only one) component on the window has the focus. This is usually indicated by a thicker border around the control, by highlighting or by the appearance of a cursor in edit boxes.

When the user presses the **[Tab]** key, the focus moves from one component to the next. The order in which the focus moves is determined by two properties: **TabStop** and **TabIndex**. The TabStop setting specifies whether or not the component can have the focus (a setting of True if it can), while TabIndex gives the order in which the components have the focus. Each component on the form has a unique tab index number.

To change the tab order, change the TabIndex setting for a component. All the index numbers will be updated to take account of the new order. For example, if there are four components on the form, the index numbers will be 0, 1, 2 and 3. To move the last component into second place, change its index number from 3 to 1. The system will then renumber the two components in the middle from 1 and 2 to 2 and 3 respectively.

Take note

All components that can have the focus have a TabIndex number but those for which TabStop is False are ignored. No two components on a form have the same TabIndex.

Tip

Don't worry about the tab settings until the form is complete — then you can set the tab index for all the components at once, when you have a better idea of the order you want.

Visible and Enabled

The Visible property determines whether the component can be seen and Enabled decides whether it can be used. As a general rule, it is less confusing for the user if components are always visible but not necessarily enabled. When a component is not enabled (its Enabled setting is False), any text displayed on it is grey and clicking on the component has no effect. Naturally, if a component is not visible (its Visible setting is False), the user cannot click on it and its Enabled property is irrelevant.

For example, you may have a Save button on your form that is enabled only when new data has been entered in edit boxes. (The alternative would be to make the Save button visible when a change is made to the data but a button suddenly popping up on the window is disconcerting for the user.)

The Visible property may be used where the value of one component affects the applicability of others. For instance, on an accounts form a pair of radio buttons may allow you to choose between a payment and a receipt. Other components on the form, such as an edit box for the cheque number, will be made visible depending on the radio button that is clicked. In another case, a command button may be clicked to display additional information on the window.

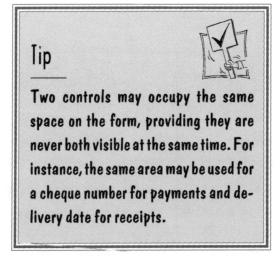

Tip

Two controls may occupy the same space on the form, providing they are never both visible at the same time. For instance, the same area may be used for a cheque number for payments and delivery date for receipts.

Standard components

The Delphi component palette contains the following Standard components:

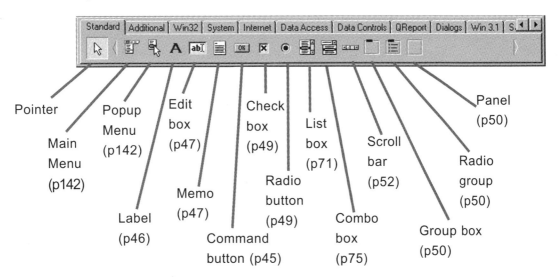

Pointer

Main
Menu
(p142)

Popup
Menu
(p142)

Label
(p46)

Edit
box
(p47)

Memo
(p47)

Command
button (p45)

Check
box
(p49)

Radio
button
(p49)

List
box
(p71)

Combo
box
(p75)

Scroll
bar
(p52)

Group box
(p50)

Panel
(p50)

Radio
group
(p50)

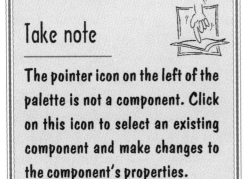

Take note

The pointer icon on the left of the palette is not a component. Click on this icon to select an existing component and make changes to the component's properties.

Other tabs on the component palette include a large number of additional components. The components that are available depend on the version of Delphi and any components that have been added. Delphi allows you to add other components using Component | Install Component. Third-party **ActiveX** components can also be added, using Component | Import ActiveX Control.

Objects

Forms and components are all **objects**. An object is self-contained; it contains both the procedures to perform its required tasks and the data that these procedures need. The procedures and data are insulated from the rest of the program; this is called **encapsulation**.

Information is passed to and from an object in the form of **messages**. For instance, when the user clicks on a button, Windows sends a message to the button object. The button carries out the required task and then sends a message back to say it has finished.

All objects of the same type come from the same **class**. For instance, all command buttons come from a class called TButton. (In Delphi, all classes begin with 'T'.) The class is a template for objects of that type.

The properties for an object are part of the date encapsulated within it. Therefore, two objects from the same class can have a different appearance because their properties have different settings.

When a class has been defined, a new class can be derived from it. Initially, the new class will have all the procedures and data from the original class; this is called **inheritance**. However, some of the procedures and data may change, giving objects from the new class different behaviour and appearance to those of the original class.

For example, TButton (the command button) is derived from a general class of controls called TButtonControl; it has all the features of TButtonControl but modifies some of these to produce a command button. Similarly, TRadioButton is also derived from TButtonControl but modifies it in a slightly different way to produce a radio button. Therefore, TButton and TRadioButton share a great many characteristics but have their own unique features; this is known as **polymorphism**. An object's class is shown at the top of the Object Inspector.

All classes are derived from a single class, called TObject, and together they form the **class hierarchy**. A small part of this hierarchy is illustrated on the left.

```
TObject
    └── TComponent
            ├── TApplication
            ├── TCommonDialog
            │       ├── TFontDialog
            │       ├── TOpenDialog
            │       └── TPrintDialog
            └── TControl
                    ├── TSpeedButton
                    └── TWinControl
                            ├── TButtonControl
                            │       ├── TButton
                            │       └── TRadioButton
                            ├── TCustomEdit
                            │       └── TEdit
                            └── TScrollingWinControl
                                    └── TCustomForm
                                            └── TForm
```

Command buttons

Command buttons are used for performing actions. A procedure is attached to each command button and is executed when the user clicks on the button. You cannot decide the order in which buttons are clicked but you do have full control over the action taken once the user has clicked a button.

The text that appears on the top of the command button is held in the **Caption** property.

The **Default** property identifies the button that will be activated when the user presses the **[Enter]** key; usually this is the OK button. Only one button on a form may have a Default setting of True; all others must be False.

In a similar way, only one button may have its **Cancel** property set to True; this is the button that will be activated when the user presses the **[Esc]** key (usually the button with a Caption of 'Cancel').

The **ModalResult** property is used when a form is opened as a **modal** window (see page 68). If you want a modal window to be closed when the button is clicked, set the **ModalReult** property to a value other than mrNone. For instance, for an OK button set it to mrOK. When the button is clicked, the form is closed and the ModalResult value can be used by a program to determine which button was used.

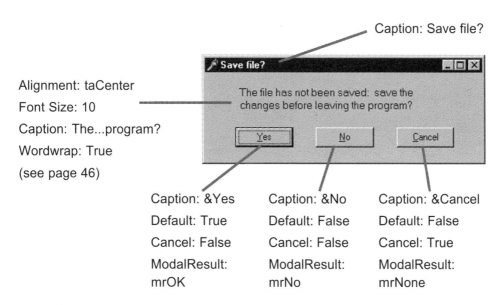

Caption: Save file?

Alignment: taCenter
Font Size: 10
Caption: The...program?
Wordwrap: True
(see page 46)

Caption: &Yes
Default: True
Cancel: False
ModalResult:
mrOK

Caption: &No
Default: False
Cancel: False
ModalResult:
mrNo

Caption: &Cancel
Default: False
Cancel: True
ModalResult:
mrNone

Labels

The **label** component adds text to the form: titles, instructions, text for data entry boxes and so on. The user cannot do anything with these components but you may wish to change the text itself at run time; for example, after a file has been selected a label may be used to display the filename.

The text of the label is held in the **Caption** property. The position of the text within the area marked out for the label is set by the **Alignment** property: taLeftJustify (left-aligned), taCenter (centred) or taRightJustify (right-aligned). The **Layout** property puts the text at the top, bottom or middle of the label area.

If the text will not fit in the label area, setting **AutoSize** to True allows the label to expand its area if necessary; for centred text, set AutoSize to False. If you want the text of the label to spread over more than one line, set **WordWrap** to True; the label will expand downwards as the length of the text increases. Otherwise, if WordWrap is False, the label expands horizontally to fit the Text.

To draw a box around the edge of the label area, change the **BorderStyle** property to 1.

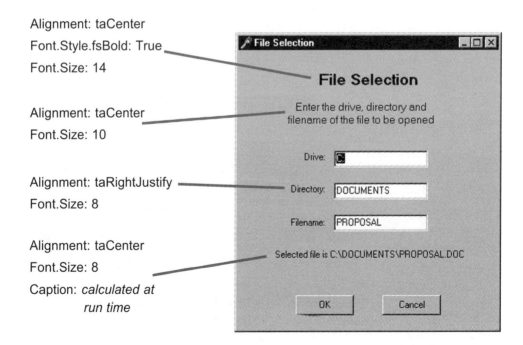

Alignment: taCenter
Font.Style.fsBold: True
Font.Size: 14

Alignment: taCenter
Font.Size: 10

Alignment: taRightJustify
Font.Size: 8

Alignment: taCenter
Font.Size: 8
Caption: *calculated at run time*

File Selection

File Selection

Enter the drive, directory and filename of the file to be opened

Drive: C

Directory: DOCUMENTS

Filename: PROPOSAL

Selected file is C:\DOCUMENTS\PROPOSAL.DOC

OK   Cancel

Edit boxes and memos

The **edit box** component provides the simplest method for the user to enter data. When the component has the focus, a vertical cursor is displayed and the user can make an entry.

The **Text** property contains the user's entry when it is complete; by setting this property during development you can supply a default value, which the user can either leave as it is or change. The **CharCase** property can be set to ecUpperCase or ecLowerCase to convert all text to upper or lower case respectively.

By default, the **BorderStyle** property is bsSingle, resulting in a box drawn around the edge of the text area. Change this to bsNone to remove the box. There is no Caption for a text box, so any description (usually to the left) must be supplied as a separate label control.

There is no Alignment property for an edit box. If **AutoSelect** is True, all text in the edit box is selected when the box gets the focus.

The **ReadOnly** property, if set to True, stops the user from changing the text. While the program is running, you may want to change this setting, depending on other choices that have been made on the form.

MaxLength sets a limit for the number of characters that can be entered in the box. For instance, a setting of 8 could be used when entering a DOS filename. If MaxLength is 0 (the default), the amount of text is limited only by the computer's memory.

The **PasswordChar** property is useful when asking the user to enter a password. The setting can be any single character (though it is usually *); this character will be displayed regardless of what the user types but the actual entry will be held in the Text property.

For large amounts of text spreading over more than one line, use a **memo** component. This has similar properties to the edit box. **Memos** have an **Alignment** property, with the same settings as labels, and a **WordWrap** property. Thre is also a **WantReturns** property, which allows users to press **[Enter]** to start a new paragraph (rather than activating the form's default button). Similarly, **WantTabs** insert tabs in the text instead of moving the focus to the next component. The **Text** property for a memo can only be set when

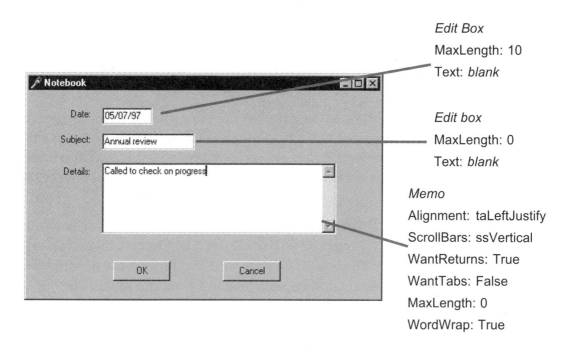

Edit Box
MaxLength: 10
Text: *blank*

Edit box
MaxLength: 0
Text: *blank*

Memo
Alignment: taLeftJustify
ScrollBars: ssVertical
WantReturns: True
WantTabs: False
MaxLength: 0
WordWrap: True

the program is running (see page 62); you can test to see if the text has changed with the **Modified** property.

In addition, the **ScrollBars** property can take the following settings:

ssNone   No scroll bars. Use when amount of text is limited.

ssHorizontal Horizontal scroll bar. The user can keep typing to the right, beyond the end of the box. Use where there are no paragraphs (e.g. for program code).

ssVertical   Vertical scroll bar. This is the most useful option, showing how much text has been typed and where the cursor is relative to the text as a whole.

ssBoth   Both scroll bars. Use this for text that can spread in both directions.

If there is no horizontal scroll bar, the text for a memo automatically wraps to the next line when the right-hand edge of the box is reached.

However, when there is no vertical scroll bar, the text will still scroll upwards when the box is full, unless you set MaxLength. Therefore, you should usually have a vertical scroll bar for a memo.

Radio buttons and check boxes

Radio buttons and check boxes provide two different methods of giving the user choices.

 Radio buttons usually appear in groups of two or more, and all the buttons on a form are interrelated (unless they are in a frame – see page 50). The component consists of a circle with a piece of text next to it. The text is held in the **Caption** property. The **Alignment** property can be taLeftJustify or taRightJustify, depending on whether the text is to be to the right or left of the circle. The**Checked** property has a setting of either True or False, depending on whether or not the button has been selected. Only one button can be selected at a time, so when the user clicks on an option button the Value for that button is set to True and for all other buttons to False.

Check boxes work in a similar way, the main difference being that they operate independently of each other. As a result, the user may select several boxes at the same time by clicking on them – or turn all boxes off. The properties are similar to those of the radio button. In addition to the usual checked/unchecked options, you can provide a third option, in which a grey tick is displayed; this is achieved by setting **AllowGrayed** to True. In this case, the type of tick is determined by the **State** property.

Tip

To make a check box temporarily unavailable, set its Enabled property to False. It is less disconcerting for a user to see a check box greyed out that for it to disappear completely (by setting Visible to False). The disabled box can be ticked by setting Check to True.

Tip

You can have more than one group of radio buttons on a window if you enclose them in frames – see below.

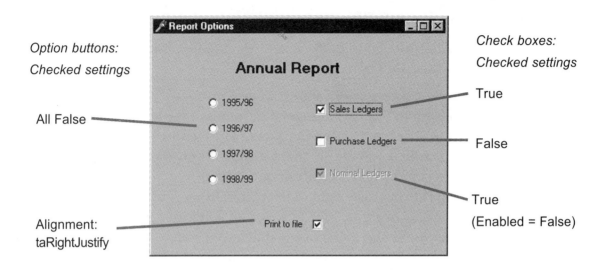

Option buttons:
Checked settings

All False ————————

Alignment:
taRightJustify ——————

Annual Report

Check boxes:
Checked settings

True

False

True
(Enabled = False)

Frames

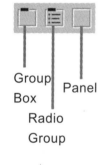

Group
Box
Panel

Radio
Group

Frames allow you to group components together. Delphi's standard components include three types of frame: radio groups, group boxes and panels.

From a functional point of view, **radio groups** are needed if you want more than one set of radio buttons on a screen. Radio buttons inside a frame act as a group, independently of any other buttons. For this to work, the radio buttons are created as part of the frame, by listing them in the frame's **Items** property; they are not created as separate components. The selected button is identified by **ItemIndex**, starting at 0 for the first item, with -1 indicating that no button is selected.

Frames can also be used to improve the appearance of the window. Apart from radio buttons, any other group of components can be placed within a **group box**, though this has no effect on the way they function. For items inside a frame, the Left and Top properties relate to the top left-hand corner of the frame.

Finally, panels can be used for splitting a window into separate areas. Strictly speaking, these are not frames, though their effect is similar. Their appearance is slightly different to that of frames.

The frame **Caption** is the piece of text overlaid on the top left-hand corner of a group box or radio group.

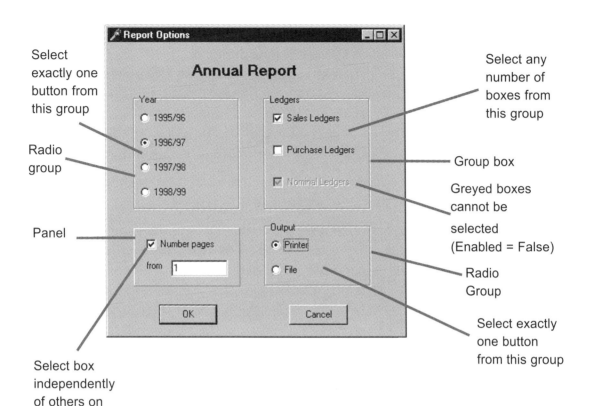

Select exactly one button from this group

Radio group

Panel

Select box independently of others on form

Select any number of boxes from this group

Group box

Greyed boxes cannot be selected (Enabled = False)

Radio Group

Select exactly one button from this group

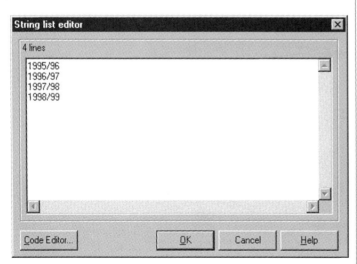

String List Editor for radio groups

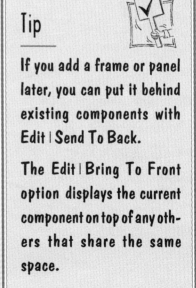

Tip

If you add a frame or panel later, you can put it behind existing components with Edit | Send To Back.

The Edit | Bring To Front option displays the current component on top of any others that share the same space.

Scroll bars

 Scroll bars frequently appear on edit boxes but you can also add them in other places. They can be added on their own (for instance, to indicate the progress of some activity or as an alternative data entry method), though standalone scroll bars tend to look rather peculiar. More usually, they can be attached to the edge of windows (for instance, one displaying part of a bitmap). In such cases, the properties are usually set while the program is running.

The direction of the scroll bar is determined by the **Kind** property: either sbHorizontal or sbVertical.

The **Min** and **Max** properties give the limits of the values that can be represented by the scroll bar; the **Position** represents the current position of the box on the scroll bar, as a proportion of the distance from one end of the scroll bar to the other. For instance, suppose that Min is 100 and Max is 200. When the box is at the top (or left) of the scroll bar, the Position is 100; when at the other end, the Position is 200; and in the middle of the bar, the Position is 150.

SmallChange specifies the amount by which Position will change when an arrow at the end of the scroll bar is clicked; **LargeChange** gives the change in Position when the bar itself is clicked (between an arrow and the scroll bar).

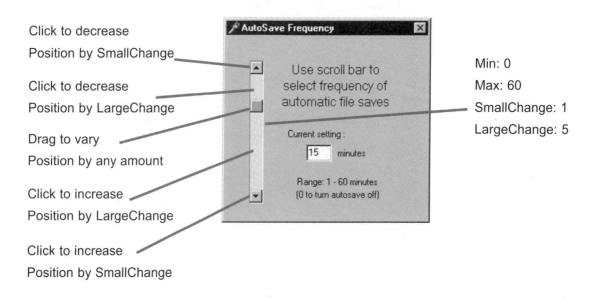

Click to decrease
Position by SmallChange

Click to decrease
Position by LargeChange

Drag to vary
Position by any amount

Click to increase
Position by LargeChange

Click to increase
Position by SmallChange

Use scroll bar to select frequency of automatic file saves

Current setting:
15 minutes

Range: 1 - 60 minutes
(0 to turn autosave off)

Min: 0
Max: 60
SmallChange: 1
LargeChange: 5

Other components

In addition to the simple components described above, a number of other components are described later:

- The **main menu** and **popup menu** add Windows menu structures to the top of the window (see page 142).

- **List** and **combo boxes** display selection lists (see page 71).

- The **image** component allows you to add bitmaps; **shape** provides simple drawing facilities (see page 170).

- The **timer** (in the System section) lets you generate events at predefined times. (Add the component to the form and then set the Interval between timer events, giving a value in milliseconds.)

- The components in the **Dialogs** section add standard Windows dialogue boxes (see page 152).

Delphi supplies many other components as standard; these tend to be more complex versions of the components already described (such as the **Mask Edit** component, which allows you to specify an input format for an edit box) or specialised components (for instance, the Internet components). You can also create your own components.

In addition to these, there are other **ActiveX** components for performing more specialised tasks. Some of these are supplied with Delphi; many others are available from third-party suppliers.

Re-running the application

You can see what your application will look like by pressing **[F9]** to run it. Clicking on a command button won't do anything but you will see the button change as it is 'depressed'. You can click on an option button, and any of the check boxes can be switched on or off.

Always save the project before running it. Occasionally, the system will 'hang' but if you have saved your work, this will not be a problem.

By this stage you should have created a fairly impressive 'front end' to your application – all without writing a line of code. Now, to make the windows and components respond to the user's actions, you need to start adding program code.

Exercises

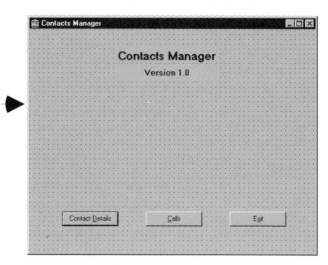

1   Add labels and command buttons to the front-end form, as shown here. The Exit button should be set up so that it is activated by pressing the **[Esc]** key.

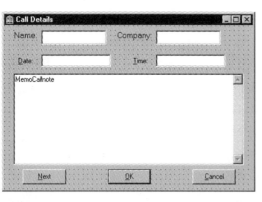

2   Create a password form. When text is typed into the edit box it should show as asterisks.

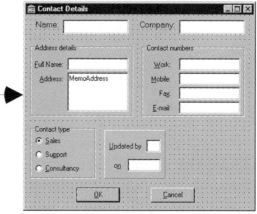

3   Add components to the Details form.

4   Add labels, edit boxes, a memo box and buttons to the Calls form.

5   Save all files and test the application.

For solutions to these exercises, see page 179.

4 Coding events

The event-led environment

In traditional programming languages, the programmer remains in absolute control when the program is run. The program consists of a linear sequence of coded instructions, with branches to particular points in the program. At each stage of the program, the user is offered a limited number of options and the program branches to the relevant section of code, according to the choice that has been made. If the code has been written correctly, there should be no surprises.

Windows programming languages, such as Delphi, start from a completely different viewpoint. At any one time there will be many **objects** on the screen: windows, buttons, menus, edit boxes and so on. The user is free to click, drag or type on any object and, in most circumstances, is not constrained to follow a linear path through a fixed sequence of actions.

This **event-led** environment requires the programmer to take a completely new approach. Rather than trying to confine the user to a limited number of actions, the programmer must create a program that reacts correctly to whatever the user does. This is not as daunting as it sounds; there are, of course, ways of limiting the user's scope (for example, making forms and controls invisible or greying out check boxes) but the simplest solution is to do nothing.

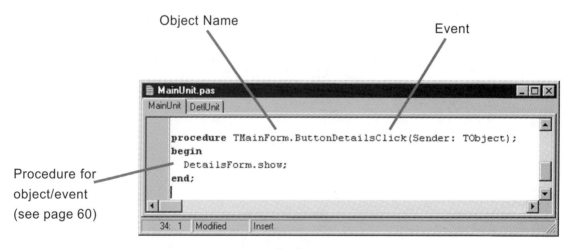

Object Name

Event

```
MainUnit.pas
MainUnit | DetlUnit |

procedure TMainForm.ButtonDetailsClick(Sender: TObject);
begin
   DetailsForm.show;
end;

34: 1    Modified    Insert
```

Procedure for object/event (see page 60)

Code window

For each object on the screen there are a number of possible **events**. Some of these are generated by the user: for instance, clicking or double-clicking the mouse-button, dragging the object or pressing a key. Others occur as a result of some other event: for example, a window opening or closing, or a component getting or losing the focus.

The code to respond to these events is contained in Delphi **procedures**. For any object, there is a procedure for each possible event; initially, every procedure is empty, so nothing happens when the event occurs. Theoretically, you could create a procedure for every event but in practice you will only fill in the procedures for those events that are of interest.

For example, a command button's events include being clicked, getting and losing the focus, and the mouse button being pressed and released. However, you may only want to provide code for the Click event; any other events would be ignored.

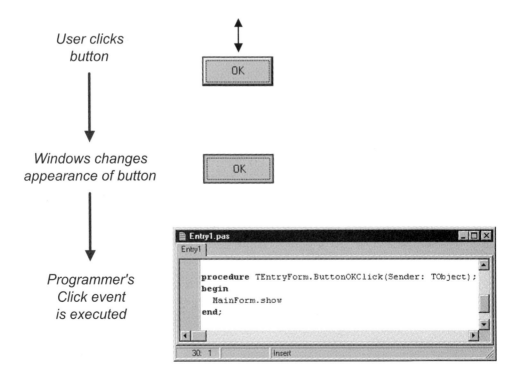

User clicks button

Windows changes appearance of button

Programmer's Click event is executed

Each event results in some action being taken by Windows itself. For instance, clicking on a command button causes it to change its appearance while the mouse button is held down; clicking on a window's Minimise button reduces the window to an icon. In these cases, you cannot alter the object's behaviour but you can add to it; for example, you may activate a new form when the command button is clicked or display a message when a form is minimised.

Therefore, the next task, after creating the user interface, is to decide the events that are to be handled and create the appropriate procedures.

Tip

Don't try to create procedures for every possible event. For each object, look through the list of events and choose the ones that are essential. You can always add new procedures later.

Take note

The command button has a Click event but you cannot double-click a button.

Common events

A number of events are common to most of the standard Delphi controls.

The **OnClick** event is generated when the user clicks the mouse button with the pointer over the object; **OnDoubleClick** occurs when the user double-clicks. For a radio button or check box, the OnClick event is also generated if you set the Checked property to True within the program.

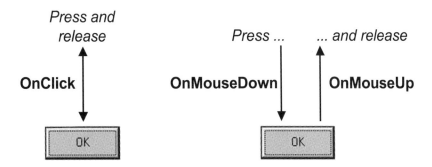

Sometimes, you may want to split the OnClick event into its two component parts: **OnMouseDown** and **OnMouseUp**. For instance, you may want to change the appearance of a component when the button is pressed and restore it when the button is released. You also need to use these events to find out which mouse button was pressed and whether the **[Shift]**, **[Ctrl]** or **[Alt]** keys were also pressed. (The OnClick event provides no extra information.)

The **OnMouseMove** event occurs when the pointer passes over the top of the object (useful for changing the appearance of the pointer at different places on the screen). **OnDragOver** occurs when an item is being dragged over the object and the **OnDragDrop** event is generated at the end of a drag operation when the mouse button is released. For these drag operations you can determine what object was being dragged, and take the appropriate action.

OnEnter and **OnExit** occur when a component gets or loses the focus, respectively. OnEnter can be used to set initial values, while OnExit is useful for checking the user's input. For example, you might use OnEnter to give an empty edit box a default value and then test the user input with OnExit; if the entry is invalid, the cursor can be put back into the edit box.

In some circumstances you may want to test for keyboard activity. **OnKeyPress** occurs when a key is pressed; this may be split into the **OnKeyDown** and **OnKeyUp** events.

You can also find out what the user has been doing by writing a procedure for an object's **OnChange** event. This event occurs whenever the value of an edit box, memo or scroll bar changes.

Creating a procedure

Procedures are created in the **code window**, which lists all the code for the current form. This window is displayed by clicking on the Toggle Unit/Form button on the toolbar or the Unit button in the Project Manager window.

Every procedure must have a name that is unique within the form. Event-driven procedures are named for you, the name consisting of the form name (prefixed with 'T'), a full stop, the component name and the event name (without the 'On' prefix). For instance, the procedure corresponding to the OnClick event for a command button called 'ButtonExit' on MainForm will be named 'TMainForm.ButtonExitClick'.

To create a procedure for an OnClick event, double-click on the component; for any other event, click on the Events tab on the Object Inspector and then double-click on the empty box to the right of the event name. Double-clicking on a blank part of a form generates the form's OnCreate event handler.

The procedure is written in the format:

```
procedure Tform.objectevent(Sender: TObject);
begin
    statements;
end;
```

The first and last lines are provided for you; all you have to do is fill in the statements in the middle. When the event occurs, the procedure statements will be executed. For example, when the user clicks on the Exit button the ButtonExitClick procedure is executed.

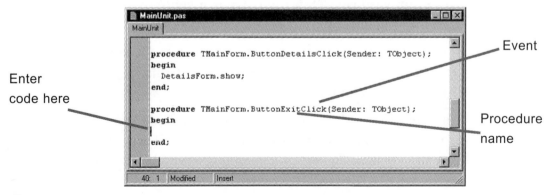

Enter code here

Event

Procedure name

Example

As an example, you can set up the Contact Details button on the front-end screen so that, when clicked, it displays the Details form. To do this you need add only a single statement to the TMainForm.ButtonContactDetailsClick procedure.

1 Double-click on the Contact Details button, so that the code window is displayed and the Click procedure is created.

2 In the blank line in the middle of the procedure type:

    DetailsForm.Show

```
procedure TMainForm.ButtonDetailsClick(Sender: TObject);
begin
  DetailsForm.show;
end;
```

3 Press **[Ctrl-S]** to save the changes.

4 Press **[F9]** to run the application. A message is displayed warning you that the form is not in the Uses list. Click on Yes and press **[F9]** again to re-run the program. (The Uses list is explained on page 78.)

5 Click on the Contact Details button. The Details form should be displayed. Close it by clicking on the Close button.

6 Select Program Reset from the Delphi Run menu to close down the application (or click on the Close button).

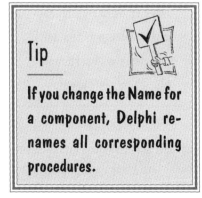

Tip

If you change the Name for a component, Delphi renames all corresponding procedures.

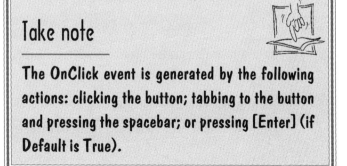

Take note

The OnClick event is generated by the following actions: clicking the button; tabbing to the button and pressing the spacebar; or pressing [Enter] (if Default is True).

Using and changing properties

You can make use of any of a component's properties when writing a procedure. You can also change most of them. The instructions to change a property must be in the format:

component.property := expression;

Component is the name you have given to the object, *property* is the Delphi property name and *expression* is any valid Delphi expression (such as a piece of text or an arithmetic calculation – see page 86). The spaces around the := symbol are optional.

Text properties

Properties such as Caption, Text and PasswordChar can only be assigned text expressions. The expression must consist of a text **string** (an actual piece of text), another text property or a combination of the two. Items of text are combined using the '+' symbol.

For example, the text for a label called LabelMessage can be changed with a statement such as:

LabelMessage.Caption := 'Please enter a value';

Any piece of text must be enclosed in a pair of single closing quotes. Similarly, the same message can be cleared by assigning the **null string** to the Caption:

LabelMessage.Caption := '';

An edit box can be given a default value with a statement such as:

LabelCountry.Text := 'UK';

A memo can be cleared with a statement such as:

MemoCallnote.Caption := '';

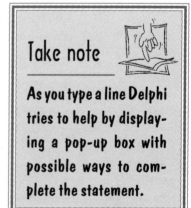

Take note

As you type a line Delphi tries to help by displaying a pop-up box with possible ways to complete the statement.

You can refer to an existing property by including it in the expression. For example, if a name is entered in a text box, the Exit event could be used for displaying the name in a label as follows:

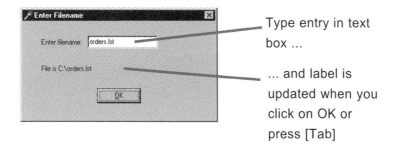

Type entry in text box ...

... and label is updated when you click on OK or press [Tab]

```
procedure TFilenameForm.EditFilenameExit(Sender: TObject);
begin
    LabelFilespec.Caption := 'File is C:\' + EditFilename.Text;
end;
```

When the user tabs to another field, the label is updated.

Numeric properties

Most properties have numeric values; for instance, Height, Width, Left, Top, BorderStyle and SmallChange are all numeric properties. These must be assigned numeric expressions, consisting of numbers and other numeric properties.

For example, the following statements change the size of a command button:

```
ButtonOK.Height := 30;
ButtonOK.Width := 80;
```

(Sizes are in pixels – see page 23.) A memo can be expanded or contracted to fit the inside of a resizable form as follows:

```
Memo1.Height := Form1.ClientHeight - 65;
Memo1.Width := Form1.ClientWidth;
```

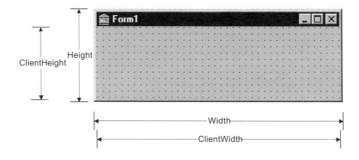

If these statements are included in the FormResize procedure, the memo will always fill the full width of the form, leaving an area at the bottom for the command buttons. The position of the command buttons can be maintained, relative to the bottom of the memo, with the statements:

```
BtnOK.Top := Form1.ClientHeight - 35;
BtnCancel.Top := BtnOK.Top;
```

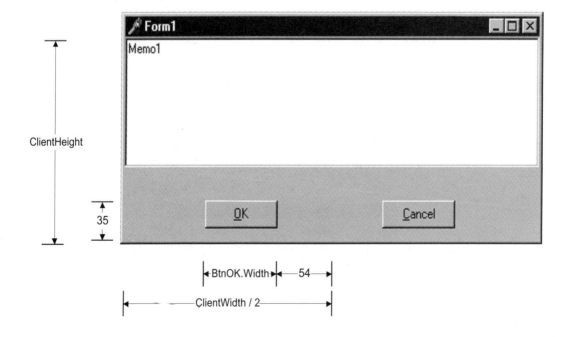

The horizontal positions of the buttons can be kept constant relative to the centre of the form with the statements:

```
BtnOK.Left := Form1.ClientWidth div 2 - 54 - BtnOK.Width;
BtnCancel.Left := Form1.ClientWidth div 2 + 54;
```

In a similar way, a form can be centred on the screen with the following statements:

```
Form1.Left := (Screen.Width - Form1.Width) div 2;
Form1.Top := (Screen.Height - Form1.Height) div 2;
```

These statements can be placed in the form's Activate procedure, which is executed when the form is first loaded.

The use of the **div** operator for division and brackets are explained on pages 86 and 87.

Take note

The Screen object has a few properties that tell you about the screen on which your program is being displayed.

You cannot change the Height and Width properties for the Screen object but you can use them in other expressions.

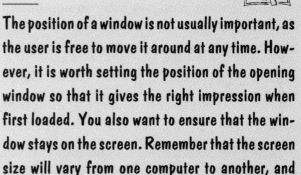

Tip

The position of a window is not usually important, as the user is free to move it around at any time. However, it is worth setting the position of the opening window so that it gives the right impression when first loaded. You also want to ensure that the window stays on the screen. Remember that the screen size will vary from one computer to another, and some screens may have a smaller display area than the machine on which the program is being developed.

Boolean properties

A number of properties can take a **Boolean** value: True or False. In such cases you can assign values of 'True' or 'False' in an expression.

For instance, a button can be disabled with the statement:

```
ButtonNext.Enabled := False;
```

When this statement has been executed, the button's caption will be greyed out and clicking on it will not generate an OnClick event.

Property references

Although most references to properties appear as *form.property* or *component.property*, there are some variations.

Within a form's procedures, you can omit the form name. For instance, the following two statements are identical:

```
Form1.ClientWidth := 285;
```

```
ClientWidth := 285;
```

However, to make your programs more easily understand, it is better to include the form name.

In the same way, all components are assumed to be on the current form. You can refer to components on other forms by prefacing the name with the form name. For instance, the following statement disables a button on a SaveData form:

```
SaveDataForm.ButtonSave.Enabled := False;
```

Using the full name you can access the properties for any components or forms included in the project.

It does no harm to include the form name, even when it is not needed. The rule is that the name may be omitted if it matches the current form.

Methods

Each object has a number of **methods** available. These are internal procedures, which can be executed from within an event-driven procedure. The methods are used for performing some action on the object. For instance, an edit box has a SetFocus method, which moves the focus to the edit box.

To execute one of these methods, it must be specified in the format:

object.method;

For example, if a value is required for a particular edit box you can force the user to make an entry with an instruction such as:

EditCompanyName.SetFocus;

As for properties and events, the methods that are available depend on the type of object.

Take note

It is important to make the distinction between properties, methods and events:

– Properties are items of information that describe a particular object (e.g. ButtonOK.TabStop determines whether pressing the [Tab] key gives the button the focus).

– Methods are built-in procedures that take some action on an object (e.g. ButtonOK.SetFocus gives the focus to the button).

– Events are user actions for which customised procedures may be written (e.g. ButtonOKEnter is executed when the button gets the focus).

Displaying forms

When you run an application, the form specified as the start-up form is loaded into memory and displayed. Other forms can be loaded and displayed using the **Show** method. For example, the following procedure loads the Details form when the Contact Details button is clicked:

```
procedure TMainForm.ButtonDetailsClick(Sender: TObject);
begin
    DetailsForm.Show;
end;
```

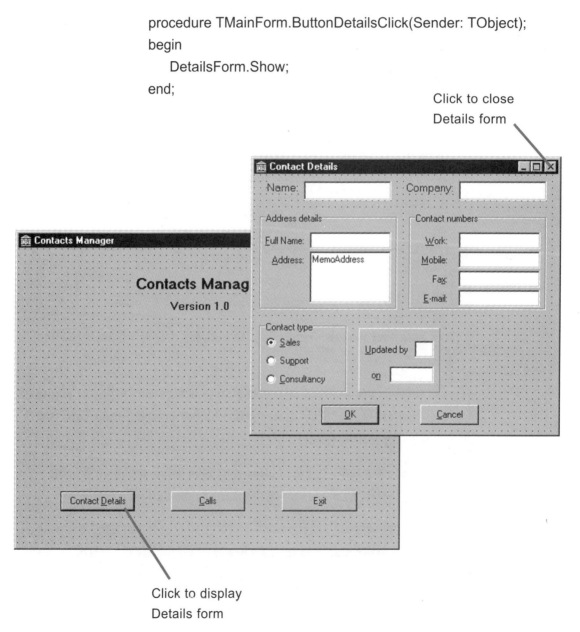

Click to close
Details form

Click to display
Details form

The start-up form

You can change the first form that is displayed using Project | Options. Click on the Forms tab and select a new Main Form from the drop-down list.

Click on
Forms tab

Click to display list of forms, then select start-up form

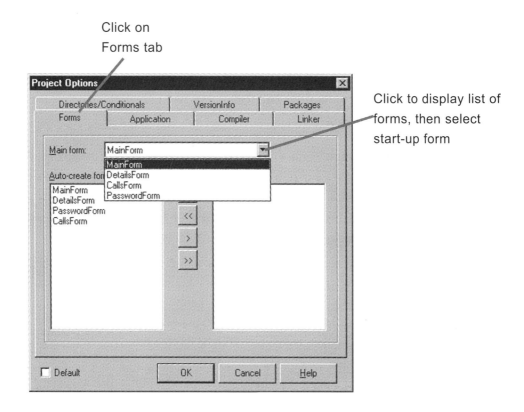

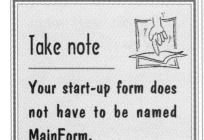

Take note

Your start-up form does not have to be named MainForm.

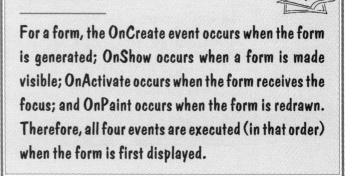

Take note

For a form, the OnCreate event occurs when the form is generated; OnShow occurs when a form is made visible; OnActivate occurs when the form receives the focus; and OnPaint occurs when the form is redrawn. Therefore, all four events are executed (in that order) when the form is first displayed.

Viewing and closing forms

A form can be hidden again with the Hide method; for example:

> DetailsForm.Hide;

This is the same as setting the Visible property to False (and executes the OnHide event). The Show method then has the same effect as setting the Visible property to True.

After a form has been hidden, it will still be held in memory. To free the memory used by the form, use the Close method; for example:

> DetailsForm.Close;

This statement removes the form from the screen, then deletes it from memory. Just before a form is closed, its OnClose event is executed. The OnClose event is also executed when the window is closed in any other way: double-clicking on the Control-menu box, clicking on the Close box or selecting the Run | Program Reset option.

Tip

Unless you want a window to remain available to the user, include a Close statement in the OnClick event for each form's 'exit' buttons (e.g. OK and Cancel). This ensures that unwanted windows are not left cluttering up the screen.

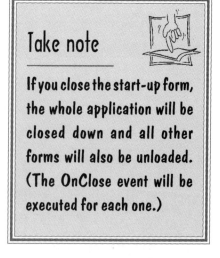

Take note

If you close the start-up form, the whole application will be closed down and all other forms will also be unloaded. (The OnClose event will be executed for each one.)

Lists

Two types of control are used for selecting an item from a list. The choice of control depends on the options you want the user to have.

List boxes

The **list box** allows the user to select from a list of options. The box consists of a rectangle containing a list of items, with a vertical scroll bar on the right-hand side (if the list is too long to fit in the box). The size of the box is specified when you add it to the form (though you can change this by varying the Height and Width properties while the program is running).

The **Items** property lists the items in the box and can be amended in the same way as for radio groups. Items can be added to the list at run time using either the **Add** method or the **Insert** method. These take the form:

> *listbox*.Items.Add(*listitem*);

> *listbox*.Items.Insert(*index, listitem*);

The *listitem* is the text item to be added to the list; *index* specifies the position for the new item in the list (starting at 0 for the item at the top of the list). For example:

> ListEurope.Items.Add('France');

> ListEurope.Items.Add(3, 'Germany');

The first statement adds the item 'France' to the bottom of the list; the second statement adds 'Germany' as the fourth item in the list.

As an alternative to specifying the index number, setting the list box's **Sorted** property to True ensures that the items are listed in alphabetical order.

When a list box has been filled, the **Items.Count** property gives you the number of items in the list. The **ItemIndex** property returns the index number of the item that is currently highlighted. If no item is currently selected, ItemIndex is -1. These properties are available only at run time.

You can refer to an item in the list by specifying the Items property with the index number in square brackets; for example:

    Edit1.Text := List1.Items[2];

    Edit1.Text := List1.Items[List1.ItemIndex];

In the first case, the edit box contains the third item in the list; in the second, the box contains the item that is currently selected.

An item can be removed from the list using the **Items.Delete** method, which takes the form:

    listbox.Items.Delete(*index*);

For example, the following statement deletes the fourth item in a list:

    ListOrgTypes.Items.Delete(3);

MultiSelect and **ExtendedSelect** allow you to select more than one item in the list:

● If MultiSelect is True but ExtendedSelect is False, several items can be selected. Clicking on an item selects or deselects it.

● If both properties are True, a series of items can be selected by clicking on the first item, holding down **[Shift]** and clicking on the last item. Individual items can be selected by holding down **[Ctrl]** while clicking.

The **Columns** property sets the number of columns in the list. The default is 0, indicating that it is a single-column list with a vertical scroll bar. For a value of 1 or more, the specified number of columns is displayed, with further columns accessed via a horizontal scroll bar.

If you want the list to display only whole items, set **IntegralHeight** to True; the box will be resized vertically so that it fits an exact number of items.

The procedures below illustrate the selection of a country from a list.

List box – filled when form is loaded

Double-click an item to activate ButtonSelectCountryClick procedure

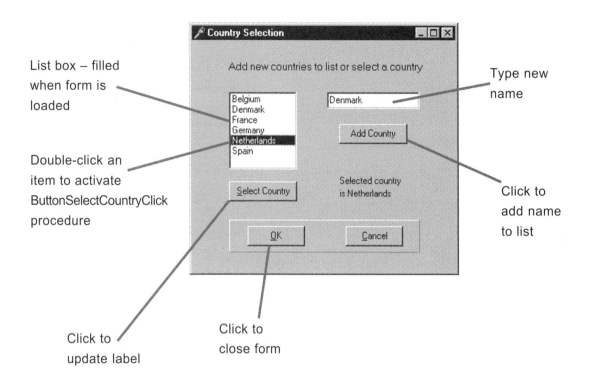

Type new name

Click to add name to list

Click to update label

Click to close form

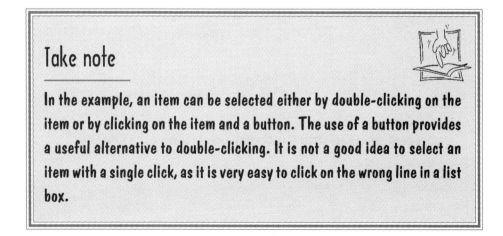

Take note

In the example, an item can be selected either by double-clicking on the item or by clicking on the item and a button. The use of a button provides a useful alternative to double-clicking. It is not a good idea to select an item with a single click, as it is very easy to click on the wrong line in a list box.

```
procedure TEuForm.FormCreate(Sender: TObject);
begin
  ListEurope.Items.Add('France');
  ListEurope.Items.Add('Germany');
  ListEurope.Items.Add('Belgium');
  ListEurope.Items.Add('Spain');
  ListEurope.Items.Add('Netherlands');
end;

procedure TEuForm.ButtonSelectCountryClick
                            (Sender: TObject);
begin
  LabelSelCountry.Caption :=
   'is ' + ListEurope.Items[ListEurope.ItemIndex];
end;

procedure TEuForm.ListEuropeDblClick
                            (Sender: TObject);
begin
  ButtonSelectCountryClick(Sender);
end;

procedure TEuForm.ButtonAddCountryClick
                            (Sender: TObject);
begin
  ListEurope.Items.Add(EditAddCountry.Text);
end;

procedure TEuForm.ButtonOKClick(Sender: TObject);
begin
  CountryForm.Close;
end;
```

Procedure names are highlighted in bold text for ease of identification.

Long statements can be split over two or more lines; the semi-colon identifies the end of the statement.

Combo boxes

A **combo box** is a combination of an edit box and a list box. An item can be selected from the list by clicking on an item or by typing an item name in the edit box at the top of the control. Depending on how the combo box is set up, the user may also be able to type new values in the edit box; these are then added to the list.

The operation of a combo box is controlled by the **Style** property, which may take the following settings:

csDropDown Clicking on the arrow makes the list drop down. An item can be selected by clicking or typing in the edit box. New items can be inserted in the edit box.

csSimple Similar to **csDropDown** but the list is displayed at all times. The height of the list is specified at design time.

csDropDownList Clicking on the arrow makes the list drop down. An item can only be selected by clicking on it.

The properties for combo boxes are similar to those for list boxes but the following points should be noted:

● For csDropDown and csSimple styles, a **Change** event is generated when the entry in the edit box is edited. The **ItemIndex** property is set to –1 for new entries.

● For the csDropDownList style, the **DoubleClick** event is not valid.

Combo boxes are useful where you want to give the user the option of extending the list. They also take up less space on the form than a simple list box.

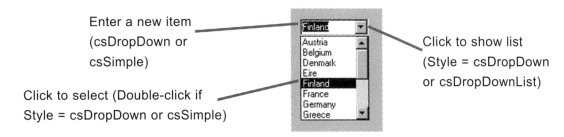

Enter a new item (csDropDown or csSimple)

Click to show list (Style = csDropDown or csDropDownList)

Click to select (Double-click if Style = csDropDown or csSimple)

Dealing with errors

Various errors may occur while you are creating procedures and running the application.

- In some cases, Delphi will correct the error for you (for instance, if an undefined form is referenced, Delphi offers to add it to the Uses list). However, most errors result in a message at the bottom of the window, with the offending line highlighted. The nature of the error is not always clear from the error message!

- If you run the application and an error is found – for example, a statement contains a reference to a form that doesn't exist – then a message box will be overlaid, specifying the nature of the error. If you click on Debug, the Code window will be displayed, with a box around the error. After correcting the error, you can either continue running the program by pressing **[F9]** or end the program with Run | Program Reset.

For more information on handling errors, see Chapter 7.

Invalid line shown
in different colour

*Error while attempting to
run the application*

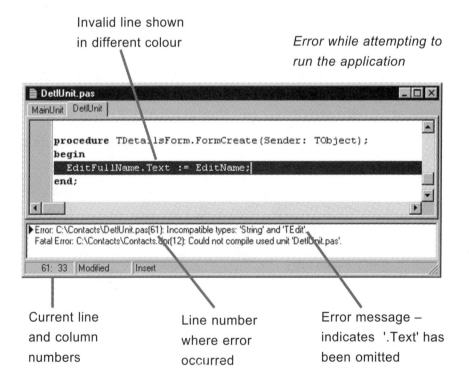

Current line
and column
numbers

Line number
where error
occurred

Error message –
indicates '.Text' has
been omitted

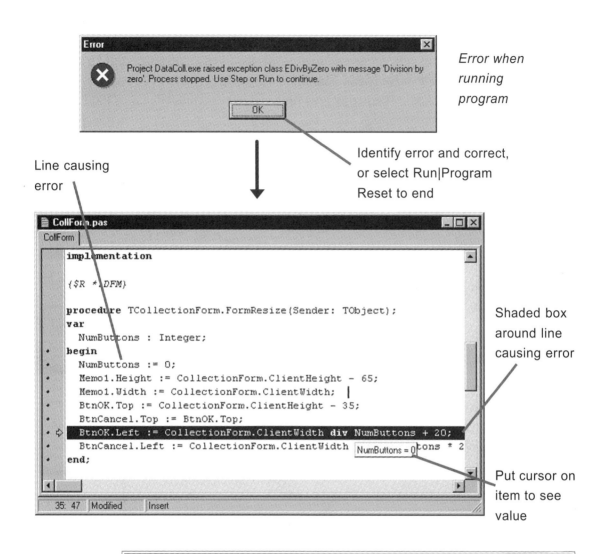

Error when running program

Identify error and correct, or select Run|Program Reset to end

Line causing error

```
  implementation

  {$R *.DFM}

  procedure TCollectionForm.FormResize(Sender: TObject);
  var
    NumButtons : Integer;
• begin
•   NumButtons := 0;
•   Memo1.Height := CollectionForm.ClientHeight - 65;
•   Memo1.Width := CollectionForm.ClientWidth;    |
•   BtnOK.Top := CollectionForm.ClientHeight - 35;
•   BtnCancel.Top := BtnOK.Top;
• ⇨ BtnOK.Left := CollectionForm.ClientWidth div NumButtons + 20;
•   BtnCancel.Left := CollectionForm.ClientWidth   NumButtons = 0 tons * 2
• end;
```

Shaded box around line causing error

Put cursor on item to see value

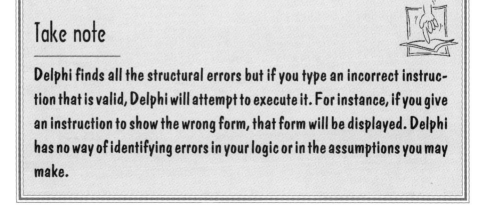
77

Program structure

Each form has a Pascal unit, containing the code needed to display and operate the form. The following code, for the MainForm, is held in the file MainUnit.pas and illustrates the structure of a Pascal unit.

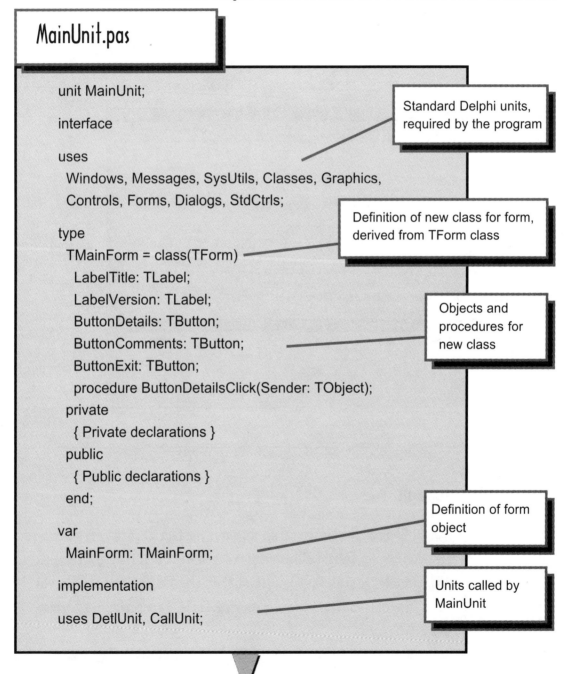

MainUnit.pas

```
unit MainUnit;

interface

uses
    Windows, Messages, SysUtils, Classes, Graphics,
    Controls, Forms, Dialogs, StdCtrls;

type
    TMainForm = class(TForm)
        LabelTitle: TLabel;
        LabelVersion: TLabel;
        ButtonDetails: TButton;
        ButtonComments: TButton;
        ButtonExit: TButton;
        procedure ButtonDetailsClick(Sender: TObject);
    private
        { Private declarations }
    public
        { Public declarations }
    end;

var
    MainForm: TMainForm;

implementation

uses DetlUnit, CallUnit;
```

Standard Delphi units, required by the program

Definition of new class for form, derived from TForm class

Objects and procedures for new class

Definition of form object

Units called by MainUnit

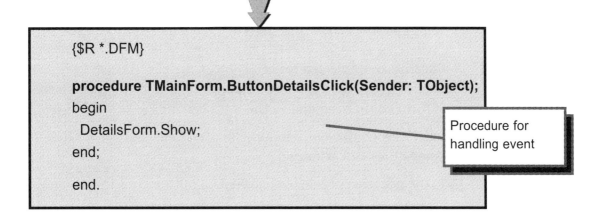

```
{$R *.DFM}

procedure TMainForm.ButtonDetailsClick(Sender: TObject);
begin
  DetailsForm.Show;
end;

end.
```

Procedure for handling event

The program is in two sections. The Interface section specifies other units that are referenced, and identifies objects, procedures and variables that are used in the program. For information on objects and classes, see page 44.

The Implementation section contains the code itself. Each procedure must have a corresponding entry in the Interface section.

Executable files

Up until this point, the program has been run from within Delphi by pressing **[F9]**. As your program begins to develop, you can also test it as a standalone EXE program (which can be run directly from Windows). The EXE program is created in the project directory every time you run the application.

You can now create an icon on the desktop for this program (using the usual Windows options) and run the program without having Delphi running at the same time.

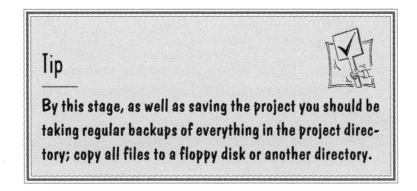

Tip

By this stage, as well as saving the project you should be taking regular backups of everything in the project directory; copy all files to a floppy disk or another directory.

Exercises

1   Using the example from the Chapter 3 Exercises, modify the OnClick procedure for the Contact Details button on the front-end form so that it displays the Details window.

2   Modify the OnClick procedure for the Calls button so that it displays the Calls window.

3   Add the necessary code so that the Exit button ends the program.

4   Add suitable code to centre the front-end form when it is first loaded.

5   Add a combo box to the Contact Details form so that the organisation type can be selected from Company, Council, Educational, Consultant, Private and Other.

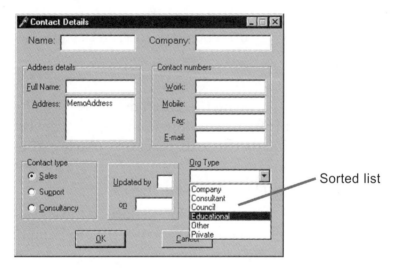

Sorted list

6   Adapt the OK and Cancel buttons on the Details form so that both return the focus to the front-end form (and close the Details form).

7   Modify the Calls form so that the edit box expands when the window is resized, leaving enough space at the bottom for the buttons.

8   Adapt the OK and Cancel buttons so that they close the Calls form and return you to the front-end form.

For solutions to these exercises, see page 183.

5 Variables

Numeric variables

While an application is running, you will want to store information temporarily. For example, if a set of statements is to be processed a number of times you need to hold the repeat number and update a count each time the loop is completed; when users enter information in edit boxes, this new data may have to be stored somewhere until you use it. All this information is stored in **variables**.

A variable is simply a named location in memory where a single item of data is held. Variables are created by being **declared** within a procedure or form. They can then be given values and these values can be retrieved or changed.

As for properties, variables fall into two broad categories:

- **Numeric variables** hold whole numbers, decimals, currency amounts, date values and the settings for numeric properties.

- **String variables** hold items of text and labels, and the settings for text properties.

You cannot mix different types; for instance, a numeric variable cannot hold a text string unless it has been converted to a number.

Variable names

Names must follow these rules:

- A variable name can be up to 63 characters long, consisting of letters, numbers and the underscore character.

- The name must start with a letter or an underscore character.

- There must no spaces or other symbols in the name.

- Upper and lower case letters are treated as being the same.

- You must not use **reserved** words (names that have a special meaning within Delphi, such as If and Unit). Search for 'Reserved words and standard directives' in the on-line help to get a list. Reserved words are shown in bold type in the code window.

- Avoid other Delphi words, such as Integer and Screen.

- All names must be unique within the project as a whole.

You should choose sensible names for your variables; programs are much more readable if names are meaningful. The aim should be to create a set of names whose content is reasonably obvious: for example, CurrentDate and AddressLine1. The use of capitals helps distinguish separate words within the name; for example, 'LastTypeToProcess' is more easily understood than the equivalent 'lasttypetoprocess'.

Declaring variables

Before you can use a variable it must be **declared**. A declaration is a statement specifying the name of a variable and its type.

The point at which a variable is declared determines its **scope**: the scope of a variable affects where else in the project it may be used:

- **Local variables**, declared at the start of a procedure (before the Begin statement), are available only within that procedure.

- **Unit-level variables**, declared at the top of the Implementation section, are available to all procedures in the form. The declaration must come after the {$R*.DFM} directive.

Variables are declared using the **Var** keyword as follows:

```
var
    variable : type;
```

You can list several variables of the same type on each line, separating them with commas. The Var section can include any number of declarations. For example:

```
var
    DayStart, DayEnd: Integer;
    FullName: string;
    NumContacts: Integer;
```

> **Take note**
>
> Properties can be thought of as predefined variables attached to particular objects; the property settings are the variable values.

In this example, three integer variables and one string variable have been declared.

The *type* can be any of the following:

Type	Bytes	Use
Boolean	1	Values that can be either True or False
Byte	1	Whole numbers in the range 0 to 255
Word	2	Whole numbers in the range 0 to 65535
ShortInt	1	Whole numbers in the range -128 to 127
SmallInt	2	Whole numbers in the range –32,768 to +32,767
Integer*	4	Very large whole numbers (±2,000,000,000)
Currency	8	Numbers with up to 4 decimal places
Single	4	Floating-point (decimal) numbers with up to 7 significant figures
Double	8	Floating-point numbers, up to 15 sig. figs.
Char*	1	A single character
String	**	Text values
Variant	***	Capable of holding any type of value

*	The size of Char and Integer variables may vary in other implentations of Pascal
**	Strings require 1 byte per character
***	Variant values require 16 bytes plus extra 1 byte per character

Floating-point numbers are also referred to as **real** numbers. Other types are also available for very large numbers or for compatibility with other versions of Pascal.

When declaring a variable, use a type from as high in this list as possible. For instance, if you know that a value will always be a whole number, choose Integer in preference to Double; if the value will always be in the range 1–100, choose Byte. The types higher in the list use less memory and programs containing them will run faster.

Constants

Some variables have fixed values that cannot be changed, either by the user or a procedure. These can be declared as **constants** using the **Const** keyword.

● Constants declared in a procedure are local to that procedure.

● Constants declared in the Implementation section of a unit are available throughout the unit.

Constant declarations take the form:

const

variable = *expression*;

Only one variable can be declared on each line and you must use '=' rather than ':='. The type of the constant depends on the *expression* that you specify.

Constants help to make your program easier to understand. They also reduce the risk of things going wrong, since the value of a constant cannot be changed inadvertently.

Tip

Use constants when the same value is needed in several places in the program; if you have to change the value later, only the Const declaration needs to be updated.

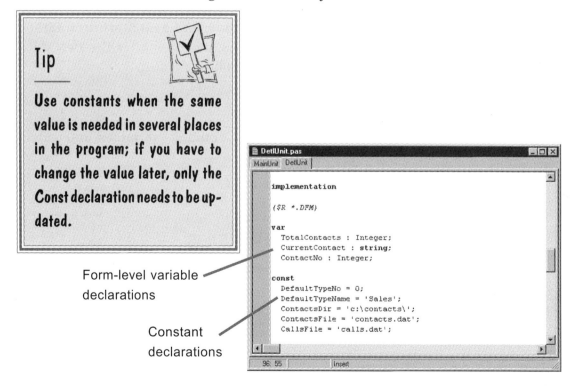

Form-level variable declarations

Constant declarations

Expressions

Values are assigned to variables using **expressions**. Such statements take the form:

> *variable* := *expression;*

The expression can be either a specific value or a combination of variables and values, linked together by **operators**. For example:

> FirstPage := 1;
> LastPage := FirstPage + 24;

In the first case, the variable FirstPage is given an explicit value of 1. In the second case, 24 is added to the value of FirstPage and the result is stored in LastPage; so if FirstPage is 1, LastPage will be 25. The value of the variable on the left of the expression is always changed by the statement; any variables in the expression itself are never changed.

Variables can also refer to themselves, as in this example:

> StockIn := 32;
> CurrentStock := CurrentStock + StockIn;

The value of StockIn (32) is added to the existing value of CurrentStock. So, if CurrentStock was originally 68, its value after the two statements have been executed will be 100.

Numeric operators

For numeric expressions, you can combine variables and values using the following operators:

*	Multiplication (e.g. 6 * 7 is 42)
/	Division (e.g. 14 / 5 is 2.8)
div	Integer division (e.g. 14 div 5 is 2)
mod	Remainder (e.g. 14 mod 5 is 4)
+	Addition
–	Subtraction

Where an expression contains more than one operator, the calculation is not done from left to right but according to the following **order of precedence**:

–	Negation (when the operator starts the expression; e.g. –2)
* / **div mod**	Multiplication and division
+ –	Addition and subtraction

When consecutive operators are at the same level, the calculation is done left to right. For example:

$$137 - 6 / 2 * 3$$
$$= 137 - 3 * 3$$
$$= 137 - 9$$
$$= 128$$

However, to avoid confusion, it is better to use brackets.

Brackets

Inserting brackets in an expression changes the order of calculation. Anything inside a pair of brackets is calculated first. Brackets must always be in matching pairs. Use only round brackets ( ), not square brackets [] or braces {}.

If brackets are nested – one pair inside another – the calculations start with the innermost pair of brackets and work outwards. For example:

$$8 + (3 * (10 / 2 - 3)) * (3 * (10 / 2 - 3))$$
$$= 8 + (3 * 2) * (3 * 2)$$
$$= 8 + 6 * 6$$
$$= 44$$

It is usually better to split complex expressions over two or more lines.

The calculation above could have been completed with the following statements:

```
NumEntries := 2;
Allocation := 10 div NumEntries – 3;
NumUnits := 3 * Allocation;
FloorSpace := NumUnits * NumUnits;
TotRequirement := FloorSpace + 8;
```

This may be more long-winded but it is easier to track down an error in the calculation and the use of variables adds meaning to the values.

The following program demonstrates the use of some simple expressions.

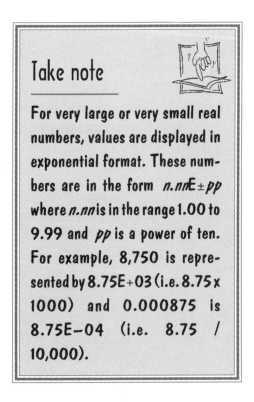

Take note

For very large or very small real numbers, values are displayed in exponential format. These numbers are in the form *n.nn*E±*pp* where *n.nn* is in the range 1.00 to 9.99 and *pp* is a power of ten. For example, 8,750 is represented by 8.75E+03 (i.e. 8.75 x 1000) and 0.000875 is 8.75E–04 (i.e. 8.75 / 10,000).

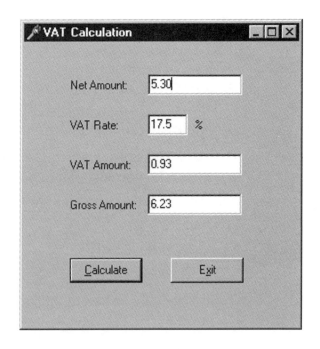

VAT Calculation

```
implementation

{$R *.DFM}

const              {Declare constants for use in whole unit}
    VATPercentage = 17.5;
    VATRate = VATPercentage /100;

procedure TVATForm.FormCreate(Sender: TObject);
begin
    {Copy VAT percentage to VAT % box}
    EditVATRate.Text := FloatToStr(VATPercentage);
end;

procedure TVATForm.ButtonCalculateClick(Sender: TObject)
var                              {Declare local variables}
    NetAmount, VAT, GrossAmount : Single;
    STemp : string;
begin
    {Get amount for calculations}
    NetAmount := StrToFloat(EditNetAmount.Text);
    VAT := NetAmount * VATRate;          {Calculate values}
    GrossAmount := NetAmount + VAT;
    Str(VAT:12:2, STemp);          {Put results in text boxes}
    EditVATAmount.Text := Trim(STemp);
    Str(GrossAmount:12:2, STemp);
    EditGrossAmount.Text := Trim(STemp);
end;

procedure TVATForm.ButtonExitClick(Sender: TObject);
begin
    VATForm.Close;
end;

end.
```

Anything in braces {} is a comment and is ignored by the program.

FloatToStr converts a real number to a string – see page 95.

StrToFloat converts a string value to a number – see page 95.

Str converts a real number to a string in a particular format.

Trim removes unnecessary spaces.

String variables and properties

Expressions can also include string variables (for handling text) and properties, both string and numeric. However, you cannot mix numeric and string variables.

String variables

String variables are much simpler to use than numeric variables. You can assign a particular item of text to a string variable by enclosing it in single quotes. For example:

    Country := 'UK';

You can also combine strings. (This is called **concatenation**.) The + operator adds one string to another. For instance:

    FullName := FirstName + ' ' + Surname;

Here, the two parts of the name are added together with a space in the middle.

Properties

You can use properties in expressions in the same way as you would variables. The following statements place an edit box in the middle of a form, the height of the box being provided by a variable, HistHt:

    EditHistory.Height := HistHt;
    EditHistory.Top := (HistForm.ClientHeight – HistHt) div 2;

In the following statement, the contents of the edit box are replaced by the value of a string variable, HistText:

    EditHistory.Text := HistText;

Numeric expressions can only include numeric properties and string expressions can only include text properties.

Functions

Delphi incorporates a number of built-in **functions**. These are routines that carry out specific operations on one or more values and return a result. The values supplied to a function are called **arguments** and are enclosed in brackets, following the function name. Multiple arguments are separated by commas.

Each argument can be a specific value or an expression. For example, the **Int** function returns the integer part of a floating-point number:

```
LengthMetres := Int(TotalLength);
NearestInt := Int(X + 0.5);
```

In the first example, the value of TotalLength is rounded down to the nearest whole number, with the answer stored in LengthMetres. In the second case, the argument is an expression and has the effect of rounding X to the nearest whole number.

Delphi provides many other numeric functions, including:

Abs   Absolute (positive value)

Sqr   Square of value

Sqrt   Square root

Log10 Log base 10

Ln   Natural logarithm

Exp   Exponential value

Sin   Sine of angle in radians

Cos   Cosine of angle in radians

Tan   Tangent of angle in radians

ArcTan Arctangent (angle whose tangent is given)

The **Random** function generates a random number between 0 and the number given as the argument. If no argument is specified, the number generated is in the range 0 to 1. (The **Randomize** statement initialises the random number sequence.)

Various other functions are introduced in later sections and many more can be found in the on-line help.

String functions

There are also many string functions. Some of the most useful functions are those that act on one string to produce another. These include:

Copy(*string, start, length*) Returns a string of given *length* for the specified *string*, beginning at the *start* character position; if *length* is greater than the number of characters from *start* onwards, the text returned continues to the end of the string

(e.g. Copy('South', 2, 3) returns 'out'
Copy('South', 1, 2) returns 'So'
Copy('South', 4, 10) returns 'th')

Length(*string*) Returns the length of the *string*
(e.g. Length('South') is 5)

TrimLeft(*string*) Removes leading spaces from *string*
(e.g. TrimLeft(' South') is 'South')

TrimRight(*string*) Removes trailing spaces from *string*
(e.g. TrimRight('South ') is 'South')

Trim(*string*) Removes spaces at both ends of the *string*
(e.g. Trim(' South ') is 'South')

StringOfChar(*character, length*)
Creates a string of the specified *character* for the given *length*
(e.g. StringOfChar('S', 5) returns 'SSSSS')

UpperCase(*string*) Converts the *string* to capitals
(e.g. UpperCase('South') returns 'SOUTH')

LowerCase(*string*) Converts the *string* to lower case
(e.g. LowerCase('South') returns 'south')

Pos(*search, main*) Searches for the first occurrence of the *search* string in the *main* string
(e.g. Pos('u', 'South') = 3)

The programs in the remainder of this book contain many examples of these functions.

For example, the following code extracts the surname from an edit box containing a forename and full name:

```
var
    Surname: string;
    SpacePos: Integer;
begin
    SpacePos := Pos(' ', EditFullName.Text);
    Surname := Copy(EditFullName.Text, SpacePos + 1, 30);
end;
```

Make sure that you put exactly one space between the pair of quotes; otherwise, the search will not be successful.

If the search string is not found, the function returns 0. (Instead of a space in quotes, you could use a constant or Chr(32) – see page 94.)

Note that Pos distinguishes between upper and lower case letters. If in doubt, use UpperCase to convert the main string to capitals and enter the search string in upper case as well.

String procedures

Some string-handling operations are performed by built-in procedures, with the result returned as an argument of the procedure.

Delete(*string*, *start*, *length*) deletes a section of the *string*, from the *start* position for the given *length*. **Insert**(*main*, *new*, *position*) inserts a *new* string in the *main* string, in front of the character at the specified *position*. For example:

```
var
    UserCode: string;
    SpacePos: Integer;
begin
    UserCode := EditUserCode.Text;  {Code format is prefix*code}
    SpacePos := Pos('*', UserCode);
    Delete(UserCode, 1, SpacePos);  {Delete everything to *}
end;
```

String conversions

Each character in a string is represented in memory by a numeric code in the range 0 to 255. The codes used are from the **ASCII character set**. In this system, A is represented by 65, B by 66 and so on; lower-case letters start at 97, numeric digits at 48; the space character is 32. If you specify one of these codes in a string, the required character will be displayed on screen or printed.

The first 128 ASCII codes are mostly standard and should produce the same result in any character font. Codes 0–31 are used for control characters, which are often found embedded in application files. The most useful control characters are 9 (tab character), 10 (line feed), 11 (form feed) and 13 (carriage return). Codes between 32 and 126 are all printable characters.

The codes for 128 onwards are rather more variable and their interpretation depends on how the computer or printer is set up and the fonts being used. These are the **extended ASCII codes**. For example, if you create a string of box-drawing characters on one computer they may appear completely different on another screen or when printed. These characters are best avoided.

The **Chr** function returns the character whose ASCII code is given; for example, Chr(32) returns a space. The reverse of this is the **Ord** function, which converts a character to its ASCII code. So Chr(74) is 'J' and Ord('J') is 74. Examples are given below.

Variable conversions

IntToStr converts an integer (or the contents of an integer variable or expression) to a string. **FloatToStr** converts a real number to a string and there are corresponding functions for other variable types.

The **Str** procedure converts a real number to a string with a specific format. Str takes the form:

Str(*real*:*width*:*decimals*, *string*);

The *real* number is converted to a *string* of specified *width* with a fixed number of *decimals*. You can remove unwanted spaces with the Trim function. See page 89 for examples.

StrToInt and **StrToFloat** reverse the process, converting a string to a numeric value. Alternatively, use the **Val** procedure:

Val(*string, numeric, error*);

The *string* is converted to a value in a *numeric* variable; if an invalid character is found, its position is held in the *error* integer variable.

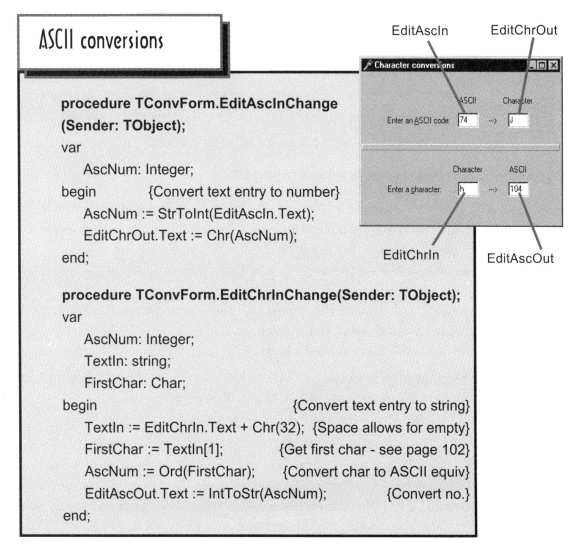

ASCII conversions

```
procedure TConvForm.EditAscInChange
(Sender: TObject);
var
    AscNum: Integer;
begin          {Convert text entry to number}
    AscNum := StrToInt(EditAscIn.Text);
    EditChrOut.Text := Chr(AscNum);
end;

procedure TConvForm.EditChrInChange(Sender: TObject);
var
    AscNum: Integer;
    TextIn: string;
    FirstChar: Char;
begin                          {Convert text entry to string}
    TextIn := EditChrIn.Text + Chr(32);  {Space allows for empty}
    FirstChar := TextIn[1];          {Get first char - see page 102}
    AscNum := Ord(FirstChar);        {Convert char to ASCII equiv}
    EditAscOut.Text := IntToStr(AscNum);          {Convert no.}
end;
```

Dates and times

The TDateTime variable type (derived from the TField class) holds a floating-point number that represents a combined date and time. The integer part of the number returns the date, representing the number of days since 30-Dec-1899. Therefore 1 represents 31-Dec-1899, 2 is 1-Jan-1900 and 36526 is 1-Jan-2000. Negative numbers give you dates before 30-Dec-1899 (and are accurate back to 1752, when the Gregorian calendar was introduced).

Take note

This is the same system that is used on Excel, Lotus 1-2-3 and other spreadsheet programs. However, some versions of Excel and Lotus are inaccurate for dates before 1-Mar-1900 and will produce different results to Delphi. (Delphi 1.0 used a different system.)

Excel and Lotus do not allow negative dates.

Excel 95 stops at 31-Dec-2078 (65380) while Lotus continues to 31-Dec-2099 (73050); Delphi and Excel 97 dates go on to the year 9999.

The decimal part of the date/time value represents the time, as a proportion of the day that has elapsed. 6 a.m. is represented by 0.25, midday is 0.5 and midnight is 0.

The combination of the two numbers gives a complete date and time; so 36526.25 represents 1-Jan-2000 6:00 a.m.

The **StrToDateTime** converts a string to a date/time value; for example, StrToDateTime('31/12/1999 6:00pm') returns the value 36525.75. **DateTimeToStr** converts a date/time value to a string in a standard format. For more control over the display format, use **FormatDateTime** which takes as its arguments a format string and the date/time value (as illustrated in the example below).

EncodeDate has a year, month and day as its arguments and returns a date/time value; similarly, **EncodeTime** has arguments of hour, minute, second and millisecond. To get the same value as the previous example you could use:

EncodeDate(1999, 12, 31) + EncodeTime(18, 0, 0,0)

DecodeDate and **DecodeTime** split a date/time value into its component parts.

DayOfWeek returns a number representing the day of the week (1 for Sunday, 2 for Monday etc.)

The **Date** and **Time** functions return date/time values representing the current system date and time respectively; **Now** returns a single value representing both date and time. There are no arguments to these functions.

The following program performs date conversions and calculations.

Tip

Use StrToDateTime when dealing with text strings entered by the user or derived from some other source; use EncodeData and EncodeTime where the separate date/time components are available.

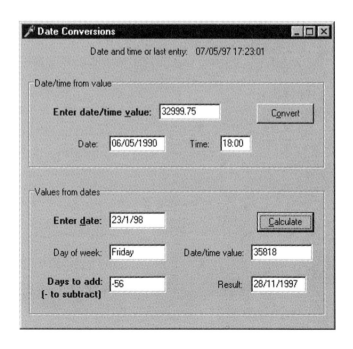

Date conversions

```
implementation

{$R *.DFM}

var
    Weekdays: array [1..7] of string;

procedure TDateForm.FormCreate(Sender: TObject);
begin
    {Set up array of weekdays}
    Weekdays[1] := 'Sunday';
    Weekdays[2] := 'Monday';
    Weekdays[3] := 'Tuesday';
    Weekdays[4] := 'Wednesday';
    Weekdays[5] := 'Thursday';
    Weekdays[6] := 'Friday';
    Weekdays[7] := 'Saturday';
end;

procedure TDateForm.ButtonConvertClick(Sender: TObject);
var
    DateOut: TDateTime;
begin
    {Convert text date/time to numeric value}
    DateOut := StrToFloat('0' + EditDTIn.Text);
    {Extract date and time and display}
    EditDateOut.Text := FormatDateTime('dd/mm/yyyy',
                                                DateOut);
    EditTimeOut.Text := FormatDateTime('hh:mm', DateOut);
    {Update main heading}
    LabelNow.Caption := DateTimeToStr(Now);
end;
```

See page 100 for a description of arrays.

The FormatDateTime function specifies the output appearance.

```
    procedure TDateForm.ButtonCalculateClick
                                    (Sender: TObject);
var
    DateIn, ResultValue: TDateTime;
begin
    {Convert text date to date/time value}
    DateIn := StrToDateTime(EditDateIn.Text);
    {Convert to string and display}
    EditDTOut.Text := FloatToStr(DateIn);
    {Calculate weekday and display}
    EditDayOfWeek.Text :=
            Weekdays[DayOfWeek(DateIn)];
    {Add/subtract number of days - must not be blank}
    ResultValue := DateIn + StrToInt(EditDaysIn.Text);
    EditResult.Text :=
            FormatDateTime('dd/mm/yyyy', ResultValue);
    {Update main heading}
    LabelNow.Caption := DateTimeToStr(Now);
    end;

    end.
```

Take note

The format string for FormatDateTime can include many different combinations of characters, allowing you to build up almost any sort of date/time display. Dates can be in numeric or text form and any part of the time can be included. For full details, search on-line help for 'FormatDateTime'.

Arrays

When handling many values or strings, the use of simple variables can be rather cumbersome. For instance, if you want to hold the values to fill a large list box you do not want a separate variable for each item, nor do you want a separate statement for adding each item to the list. You can overcome these problems by the use of arrays.

An **array** is a set of variables, represented by a single name. The individual values are called **elements** and are identified by **index numbers**. The index number is given in square brackets after the name.

For example, the array MonthDays could hold the number of days in the month; MonthDays[1] holds the number of days in January, MonthDays[2] is for February and so on to MonthDays[12], which represents the numbers of days in December.

Arrays are declared in the same way as for simple variables. You must declare the type of the array and, within the brackets, the range of index numbers is specified. For example:

```
var
        MonthDays: array [1..12] of Integer;
        InvoiceYears: array [1980..1999] of Integer;
```

This statement declares an array of 12 elements (numbered from 1 to 12), each of which can hold an integer value.

An array may have more than one **dimension**. For example:

```
var
        MaxTemp: array [1..12, 1..31] as Single;
```

Each possible combination of the two index numbers identifies a different element. In this case there are 372 single-precision values in the array, which can be used for storing the maximum temperature in each day of the year. For instance, MaxTemp[4, 17] could hold the value for 17 April.

Any element in an array can be used in an expression in the same way as for a normal variable. The *Date conversions* program on page 98 gives an example of an array for holding the days of the week.

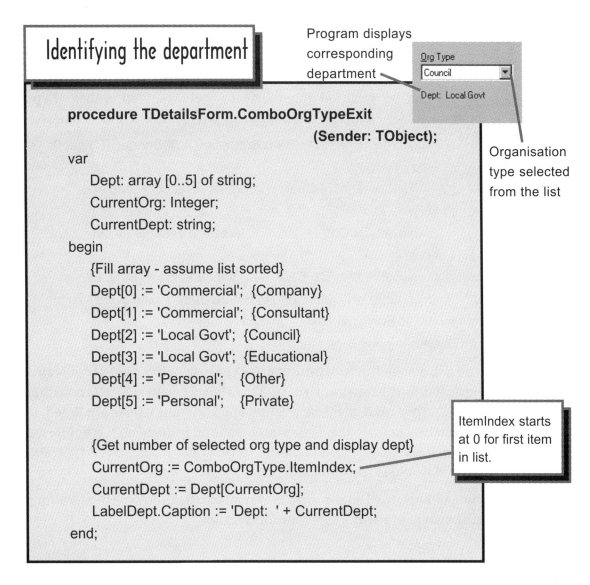

Identifying the department

Program displays corresponding department

Org Type
Council ▼
Dept: Local Govt

Organisation type selected from the list

```
procedure TDetailsForm.ComboOrgTypeExit
                        (Sender: TObject);
var
    Dept: array [0..5] of string;
    CurrentOrg: Integer;
    CurrentDept: string;
begin
    {Fill array - assume list sorted}
    Dept[0] := 'Commercial';  {Company}
    Dept[1] := 'Commercial';  {Consultant}
    Dept[2] := 'Local Govt';  {Council}
    Dept[3] := 'Local Govt';  {Educational}
    Dept[4] := 'Personal';    {Other}
    Dept[5] := 'Personal';    {Private}

    {Get number of selected org type and display dept}
    CurrentOrg := ComboOrgType.ItemIndex;
    CurrentDept := Dept[CurrentOrg];
    LabelDept.Caption := 'Dept: ' + CurrentDept;
end;
```

ItemIndex starts at 0 for first item in list.

String arrays

String variables can also be treated as arrays, in which each character is a single character. For instance, PartCode[2] represents the second character of the string PartCode.

Strings can also be declared as fixed length:

```
var
    PartCode: string[10];
```

This defines a string of exactly ten characters. The variable is used like any other string.

Sets and enumerated types

Values can be grouped together into **sets**, defined with a **Type** statement. Set elements are held in square brackets. For example:

```
procedure TEmployeeForm.ButtonOKClick(Sender: TObject);
type
    TNICat = set of Char;        {define set of characters}
var
    NICat: TNICat;               {declare variable as set}
begin
    NICat := ['A'..'C', 'F'];    {set contains A, B, C, F}
    if not(EditNICat.Text[1] in NICat) then    {see page 120 for 'if'}
        EditError.Text := 'Invalid NI Category';
end;
```

You can also define an **enumerated type**, which is a set of constants representing the integers from 0. This allows you to refer to a constant name, rather than an integer value. The constant names are listed, in normal brackets, in the Type statement and require no further declaration. Variables can be declared to be of the enumerated type and may take values from the set.

For example, the Details form may contain the following declarations at the start of the Implementation section:

```
type
    TContactType = (Sales, Support, Consultancy);
var
    CurrentContactType: TContactType;
```

The new variable can be given a value from the set when a radio button is clicked:

```
if RadioCType.ItemIndex = 0 then
    CurrentContactType := Sales;
```

Elsewhere, the variable can be tested to select the action to be taken:

```
if CurrentContactType = Sales then ...;
```

This is easier to understand than a test against a value of 0.

Message boxes

The **MessageDlg** function displays a temporary dialogue box. The box contains a line of text, an icon and one or more command buttons. The function is invoked with a statement in the following format:

variable := MessageDlg(*message, icon, buttons, help*);

The *message* is any line of text; *icon* determines the icon to be displayed and the text for the title bar; *buttons* specifies the buttons for the box; and help provides a link to a *help* file (0 for no link). Possible values are:

Icon	Buttons	
	Values:	*Sets:*
mtWarning	mbYes	mbYesNoCancel
mtError	mbNo	mbOKCancel
mtInformation	mbOK	mbAbortRetryIgnore
mtConfirmation	mbCancel	
mtCustom	mbHelp	
	mbAbort	
	mbRetry	
	mbIgnore	
	mbAll	

The value returned to the *variable* is the button that was pressed:

mrNone	mrAbort	mrYes
mrOK	mrRetry	mrNo
mrCancel	mrIgnore	mrAll

The button *values* must be in square brackets; the predefined *sets* must not. For example, to display a warning with two buttons:

Action := MessageDlg('The existing file will be replaced', mtWarning, [mbOK, mbCancel], 0);

If you do not care which key is pressed, omit the variable:

MessageDlg('The existing file will be replaced', mtWarning, mbOKCancel, 0);

The effect is the same as for the function.

Exercises

1. Create the conversion form below. When one of the buttons is clicked the value in the Entry box (on the left) should be converted into the new units and shown in the Result box (on the right), to two decimal places.

   The labels for the Entry and Result boxes should be changed to show the two conversion units. When a new entry is started, the labels should revert to their default values and the Result box should be cleared.

   The Exit button should end the program.

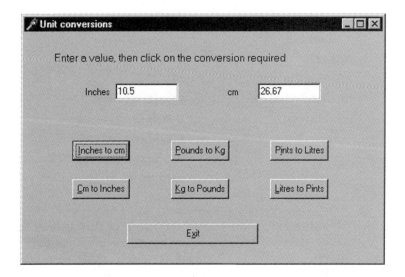

2. Add the OrgType box to the Details form (as described in *Arrays* on page 101). The Dept label should be updated as soon as an organisation type is clicked.

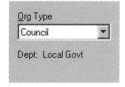

3. Write a program to calculate the number of weeks and days between any two dates.

For solutions to these exercises, see page 185.

6 Basic instructions

Units

Much of the work done by an application is performed by event-driven procedures; these provide the responses to the user's actions. However, some code will be needed for more general-purpose actions, such as reading data from a file or checking that a date is valid. This code may be put in a separate code **unit**.

Most applications will have at least one extra unit, containing procedures for performing frequently-used tasks. These procedures are called as and when needed. This has a number of advantages:

- The code has to be written only once; when it has been tested satisfactorily you will be able to use it elsewhere in the application without having to go through the coding process again.

- Since there is only one copy of the code, there is no danger that the same process somewhere else in the application will work in a slightly different way.

- If you need to make a change to the way a procedure works, this has to be done once only; there is no need to search through your code looking for other occurrences of the same code.

- Code modules can be re-used by other applications; when you have developed a set of general-purpose procedures, these can be incorporated in other projects, helping to give all your applications the same 'look and feel'.

You can have any number of code units in your project so it is a good idea to split up your general-purpose procedures. For instance, you may have one unit for text-handling procedures, another for date routines and a third for dealing with graphics.

If you decide that part of an event-driven procedure will be useful elsewhere, you can move it to a separate procedure in another unit using cut-and-paste operations.

Scope

When designing the overall structure of your application it is essential to have an understanding of the **scope** of procedures. This determines what procedures are available in any part of the application. The rules are as follows:

● If the header for a procedure is copied to the Interface section of the unit, it will be available to any other unit.

● If the procedure appears only in the Implementation section, it is available only within that unit.

If you want to make use of a procedure from another unit, you must specify that unit in a **Uses** statement at the start of the Implementation section.

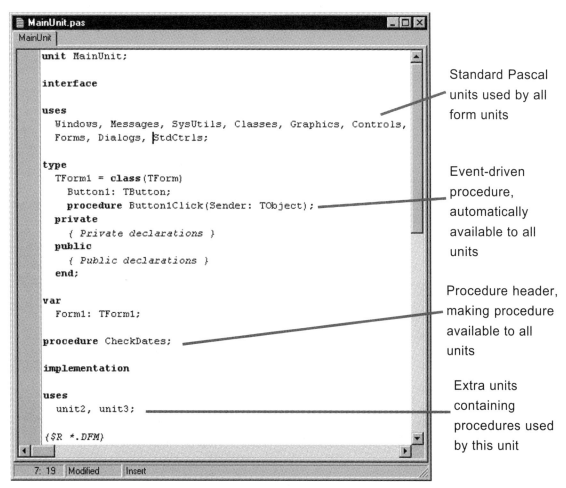

```
MainUnit.pas
MainUnit

unit MainUnit;

interface

uses
   Windows, Messages, SysUtils, Classes, Graphics, Controls,
   Forms, Dialogs, StdCtrls;

type
   TForm1 = class(TForm)
     Button1: TButton;
     procedure Button1Click(Sender: TObject);
   private
     { Private declarations }
   public
     { Public declarations }
   end;

var
   Form1: TForm1;

procedure CheckDates;

implementation

uses
   unit2, unit3;

{$R *.DFM}
```
```
7: 19    Modified    Insert
```

Standard Pascal units used by all form units

Event-driven procedure, automatically available to all units

Procedure header, making procedure available to all units

Extra units containing procedures used by this unit

Creating units and procedures

New units and procedures are created with a few simple commands.

Creating units

To create a new code unit:

1   Select File|New and double-click on the Unit icon. The code window for the new unit is displayed.

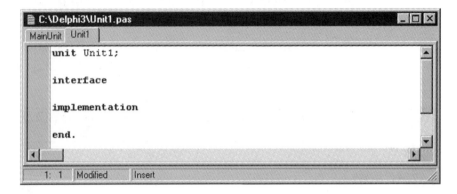

2   Select File|Save As to save the unit. Enter a valid filename and click on OK; a PAS extension will be added to the name.

Select drive and
directory

Enter a filename
(PAS extension will
be added)

Indicates that
only PAS files are
listed above

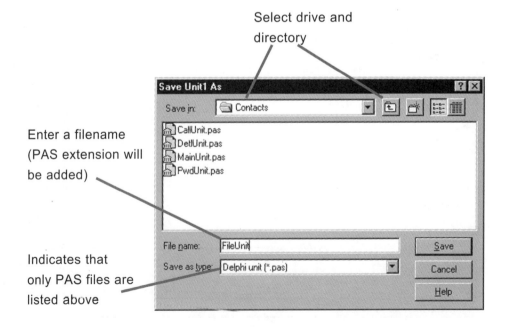

3   Save the project. The new unit is added to the Project Manager window.

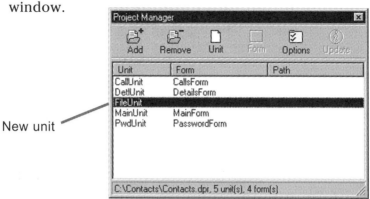

New unit

At any time, highlighting the unit name in the Project Manager window and then clicking on the Unit button will redisplay the code window.

Changing units

You can add an existing unit to the project with Project | Add To Project. Select a file with a PAS extension and click on Open. (Alternatively, use the Add button on the Project Manager window.)

To remove a unit, click on its name in the Project Manager window and then click on the Remove button.

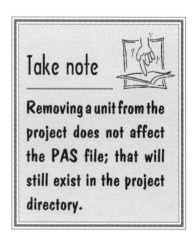

Take note

Removing a unit from the project does not affect the PAS file; that will still exist in the project directory.

Creating procedures in units

To add a general-purpose procedure to a code unit:

1   Double-click on the unit name in the Project Manager window (or click on the unit name and then on the Unit button). The code window is displayed.

Initially, the code consists of the bare minimum: the unit name, the two section headings and the 'end' statement.

109

2 Type the procedure header in the Interface section to show that the procedure is to be available throughout the project. The header consists of the word 'procedure', the procedure name (following the rules given below) and a semi-colon.

Procedure name (same rules as for variables)

Procedure header in Interface section – so available throughout project

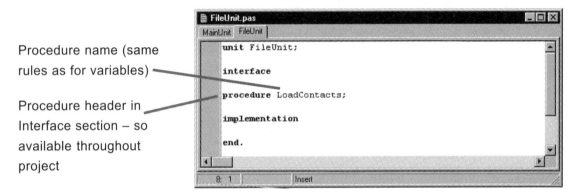

Repeat the procedure header in the Implementation section. Add the Begin and End statements below this, remembering to include a semi-colon after the End statement. Any Type or Var statements can be inserted above the Begin statement, and the procedure code itself is entered below.

Insert Var and Type statements here

Insert code here

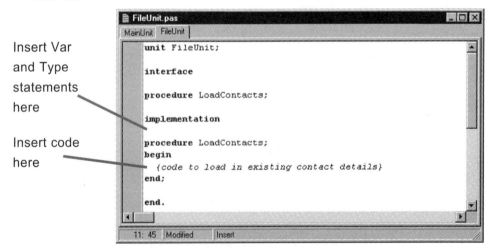

The procedure can be viewed or edited later simply by selecting the unit and then scrolling through the code window. The units that are to call this procedure must have a Uses statement that specifies the name of this unit.

Creating procedures in forms

You can also add a general-purpose procedure to a form. This is achieved in a similar way to that for procedures in extra units:

1 Click on the form name in the Project Manager window, then on the Unit button.

2 Type the procedure header in the Interface section.

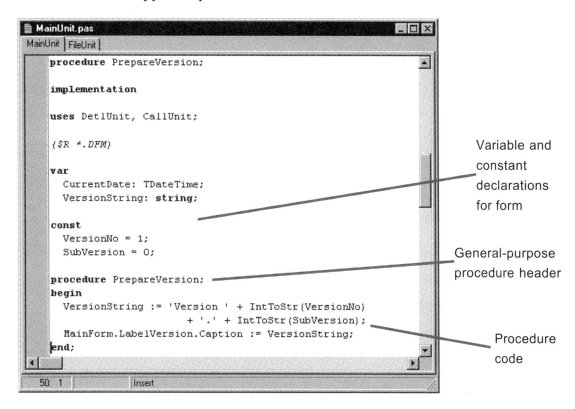

```
MainUnit.pas
MainUnit | FileUnit |

    procedure PrepareVersion;

    implementation

    uses DetlUnit, CallUnit;

    {$R *.DFM}

    var
       CurrentDate: TDateTime;
       VersionString: string;

    const
       VersionNo = 1;
       SubVersion = 0;

    procedure PrepareVersion;
    begin
       VersionString := 'Version ' + IntToStr(VersionNo)
                        + '.' + IntToStr(SubVersion);
       MainForm.LabelVersion.Caption := VersionString;
    end;

50: 1          Insert
```

Variable and constant declarations for form

General-purpose procedure header

Procedure code

3 Repeat the header in the Implementation section and enter the code below it (bracketing the code between the Begin and End statements). Any references to components must be prefixed by the form name (even if they are on the same form).

Form-level procedures are useful for routines that may be used more than once in a form but are unlikely to be needed in any other project. If the general-purpose procedure is to be used by other forms in the project, then the form name must be included in their Uses statements.

Procedure names

Event procedures are automatically named for you. Their names are not necessarily unique in the project as a whole; for example, if two forms each have a ButtonOK command button, then both will have a ButtonOKClick procedure. However, this is not a problem, since the procedure names are prefixed with the form name.

On the other hand, each general-purpose procedure in a project must be given a unique name.

The rules for naming procedures are the same as those for variables: no more than 63 characters (letters, numbers and underscores); starting with a letter or underscore; no spaces or symbols apart from the underscore. Use capital letters to identify individual words within the name; this helps to make the name meaningful.

Take note

If you change the name of a general-purpose procedure, remember to change the corresponding header in the Interface section and change any references to the procedure elsewhere in the program.

If you want to change the name of an event-driven procedure, you must do so by changing the Name property for the object; the procedure name will be updated automatically (though other references must be updated manually). Do not try to change the procedure header manually.

Deleting procedures

You can delete a general-purpose procedure by deleting it from the Implementation section. Remember to delete the header in the Interface section and revise any references elsewhere in the program.

For event procedures, delete all code between the Begin and End statements. Delphi will finish the job for you. However, you must revise any calls to the procedures elsewhere in the project.

Calling procedures

A general-purpose procedure is executed by **calling** it from another procedure. The procedure is called by entering the name on a line on its own in the code. For example, a procedure called ApplyDefaults may be used to fill the boxes on a form with default values:

```
var
    NextInvNum: Integer;

procedure ApplyDefaults;
begin
    InvoiceForm.EditDiscRate.Text := '0.10';
    InvoiceForm.EditInvoiceNo.Text := IntToStr(NextInvNum + 1);
end;
```

This procedure could be called either as part of the form's Create event or when a Defaults button is pressed on the form. For example:

```
procedure TInvoiceForm.FormCreate(Sender: TObject);
begin
    ApplyDefaults;
end;
```

As a result, the boxes are filled with the default values.

Within a general-purpose procedure, any references to components must specify the form name (even if the procedure is in the same unit as the form). You can also call an event procedure from anywhere in the project, providing you prefix it with the form name. You will need to include 'Sender' in brackets after the procedure name. For example:

```
procedure TMainForm.ButtonExitClick(Sender: TObject);
begin
    DetailsForm.ButtonOKClick(Sender);
    Mainform.Close;
end;
```

If you are calling an event procedure in the same form you can omit the form name.

Public and passed variables

When you call an event-driven procedure, no other information is needed for the procedure to be executed. However, for general-purpose procedures, you usually need to make further details available to it and the procedure will often need to pass back some result. For instance, a procedure to calculate the number of days between two dates needs to know the dates to be used in the calculation and must be able to return the answer; if a procedure is used for setting up an array, the contents of the array must be made available to other procedures. All of this is handled by the use of public variables and by passing the contents of variables to and from procedures.

Local, private and public variables

The **scope** of variables depends on where they are declared:

- Variables declared in a procedure are **local** to that procedure – they have no meaning elsewhere in the project.

- Variables declared at the top of the Implementation section (**private** variables) are available throughout the unit but not in other units.

- Variables declared in the Interface section (**public** variables) are available throughout the whole project. The value of a public variable can be used by any procedure, in any unit. For example, a user name entered on an introductory screen may be needed elsewhere in the program, so its variable must be public.

Constants can also be local, private or public, depending on where

Take note

As a general rule, you should make variables as local as possible; use local variables in preference to private variables, and private variables in preference to public variables. This reduces memory requirements and helps you to keep track of your variables and their values.

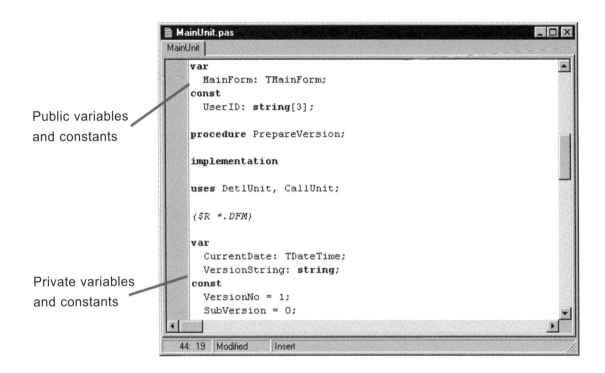

Public variables
and constants

Private variables
and constants

```
var
  MainForm: TMainForm;
const
  UserID: string[3];

procedure PrepareVersion;

implementation

uses Det1Unit, CallUnit;

{$R *.DFM}

var
  CurrentDate: TDateTime;
  VersionString: string;
const
  VersionNo = 1;
  SubVersion = 0;
```

they are declared.

Passing variables to procedures

One way of exchanging information with procedures would be to hold the values in public variables. However, it is more efficient to **pass** the values across when the procedure is called. The variables that are passed to the procedure must be declared in the Procedure statement, in brackets following the procedure name. The first line of the procedure will be follows:

procedure *procname*(*variable*: *type*, ...);

The brackets can contain more than one variable (when more than one value is passed); separate variables of the same type with commas, those of different types with semi-colons. If no variables are passed, the brackets are omitted. The brackets should also contain any variables that are to be passed back to the calling procedure.

When the procedure is called the variable values are listed in brackets following the procedure name.

For example, the following procedure extracts the house name or

```
procedure ExtractHouse(var HouseName, StreetName: string);
var
    CommaPos: Integer;
const
    Comma = ',';
begin
    {Find comma and extract everything before it}
    CommaPos := Pos(Comma, StreetName);
    HouseName := Copy(StreetName, 1, CommaPos - 1);
    {Remove house from street}
    Delete(StreetName, 1, CommaPos);
    StreetName := Trim(StreetName);
end;
```

number from the first line of an address:

Here, StreetName is used for passing a value to the procedure; the procedure uses HouseName for passing a value back and it also changes StreetName, passing back a different value.

CommaPos is a local variable, which exists only as long as the procedure is running.

By including variables in the Procedure line you are effectively declaring them as local variables for that procedure. If you want to stop a variable being changed when passed back from a procedure, remove the **Var** keyword before the variable name in the procedure definition. For example:

```
procedure ExtractHouse(var HouseName: string; StreetName:
string);
```

Here, any change to StreetName will not be passed back to the calling procedure.

The following procedure, which is invoked by clicking on a button, gets the contents of an edit box and calls the ExtractHouse procedure. The returned values are copied into two edit boxes.

```
procedure TAddressForm.ButtonExtractClick(Sender: TObject);
var
    House, Street: string;
begin                      {Get first line of address and call procedure}
    Street := EditAddressLine1.Text;
    ExtractHouse(House, Street);
    EditHouse.Text := House;    {Put results into two other boxes}
    EditStreet.Text := Street;
end;
```

The variables on the line calling the procedure do not have to have the same names as those used within the procedure itself (though they may be the same, if you wish). In the example above, the original value is passed across in the Street variable; the procedure transfers this into the corresponding StreetName local variable, which is then changed; the new value of StreetName is passed back into the Street variable. Similarly, HouseName is passed back as House.

Comments and spacing

You can make your programs more readable by adding **comments**. Although you may understand now what your program does, a few reminders might be helpful when you come to look at it again in a few months' time. Any text in braces { } is treated as a comment and is ignored by Delphi. Comments may spread over several lines.

You can also use two slashes // to mark a comment. In this case, anything afterwards, to the end of the line only, is a comment. This method is useful for temporarily removing a line of code. A larger block can be commented out with (* at the start and *) at the end.

Programs are easier to understand if they are well spaced out. Use plenty of spaces in each line and extra blank lines between sections.

User-defined functions

Delphi provides many built-in functions for handling text and numbers but there will be others that you must create yourself. One way of doing this would be to use a procedure. For example, the following procedure converts inches to centimetres.

```
procedure InchesToCmP(var Inches, Cm: Single);
const
    CmPerInch = 2.54;
begin
    Cm := Inches * CmPerInch;
end;
```

The converted value is displayed in a box with the following code:

```
Inches := StrToFloat(EditEntry.Text);
InchesToCmP(Inches, Cm);
EditResult.Text := FloatToStr(Cm);
```

However, it is often simpler to define a function for this sort of task.

User-defined functions are created in a similar way to procedures. Use **function** instead of **procedure** on the first line, specifying in brackets any variables being passed. You must also add a declaration of the function type at the end of the line. Type Begin and End lines below the function header. The function code itself is inserted above the End line. The function will return a single value, which is calculated in a variable with the same name and type as the function.

If the function is to be used by other units, add an exact copy of the function header line in the Interface section.

The following function converts inches to centimetres:

```
function InchesToCm(Inches: Single): Single;
const
    CmPerInch = 2.54;
begin
    InchesToCm := Inches * CmPerInch;
end;
```

In order to use the function, include it in a statement in the same way as for a built-in function. This function could be used to supply the value for an edit box as follows:

```
Cm := InchesToCm(Inches);
```

When this statement is executed, the InchesToCm function is called and the value of Inches is passed to it. The function calculates a value for the InchesToCm variable, and this is then slotted back into the original expression.

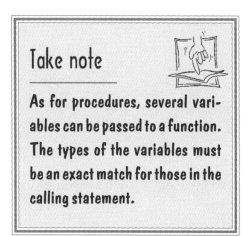

Take note

As for procedures, several variables can be passed to a function. The types of the variables must be an exact match for those in the calling statement.

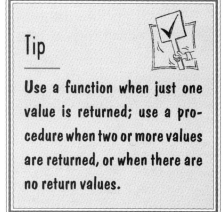

Tip

Use a function when just one value is returned; use a procedure when two or more values are returned, or when there are no return values.

The following is a particularly useful function to raise a number to a power:

```
function Power(ValueIn, Exponent: Single): Single;
{Calculate ValueIn to power Exponent
 Return -1 if ValueIn less than or equal to 0}
begin
    if ValueIn <= 0 then
        Power := -1
    else
        Power := exp(Exponent * Ln(ValueIn));
end;
```

Conditional statements

So far, the statements in a procedure have followed a linear, unbroken path; the program starts at the first line and works down through each line in turn until the last line has been completed. Procedures are rarely like this, however. Most of the time there are choices to be made and, as a result, statements to be executed only **if** a condition is true. For example, if a value entered in a text box exceeds some limit you may want to display an error message.

Such decisions are made using the **If...Then...** set of statements, which take the form:

        If *condition* then
            begin
                statements;
            end;

The *statements* are executed only if the *condition* is true. The condition usually takes the form:

        expression operator expression

Any valid expressions can be used, with the restriction that both must be of the same type.

The **operator** is one of the following:

=	Equal to
<>	Not equal to
<	Less than
<=	Less than or equal to
>	Greater than
>=	Greater than or equal to
in	Expression is in set

For example, the following procedure tests the value of an entry in an edit box when the focus is moved to another component. If the value is too high, it is replaced by the maximum allowed, a warning message is displayed and the cursor is put back in the edit box.

```
procedure TClockForm.EditMinutesExit(Sender: TObject);
begin
    if StrToInt(EditMinutes.Text) > 59 then
        begin
          MessageDlg('Minutes must be < 60', mtError, [mbOK], 0);
          EditMinutes.Text := '59';
          EditMinutes.SetFocus;
        end;
end;
```

You do not have to indent the statements below the If statement or between the Begin and End statements but it makes the code much more readable. Indenting conditional sections of code becomes important when you start to put one condition inside another.

Take note

If you are only executing one instruction, there is no need for the Begin and End statements. The whole statement can be on one line. For example:

if TotalTime < 30 then PayRate := 1;

For numeric conditions, the tests are carried out on the relative numeric values of the expressions. For string expressions, the comparisons are performed character-by-character, according to the ASCII code of the characters. The following conditions are all true:

Tip

To sort strings containing numbers into numerical order, pad the numbers with leading zeroes or spaces.

Numeric	String
-4 < 21	'B' < 'Ba'
5 < 2*3	'B' < 'a'
2.1 < 20	'2' < 'B'
3 < 21	'21' < '3'

121

You can combine string expressions with the following **logical operators**:

and   Both conditions must be true for the combined condition to be true

or   One (or both) of the conditions must be true

xor   One of the conditions must be true but not both (Exclusive Or)

Each of the conditions must be enclosed in a pair of brackets. The two sets of conditions can be either numeric or text, independently of each other. For example:

```
DaysInFeb := 28;
if (NumMonth = 2) and (LeapYearText = 'Yes') then
    DaysInFeb := 29;
```

In this case, if NumMonth is not equal to 2 or LeapYearText contains text other than 'Yes', the value of DaysInFeb would remain at 28.

You can also negate a condition by putting **Not** in front of it. For example:

```
if (not (NumMonth = 2)) and (DaysInMonth <> 31) then
    NumDays := 30;
```

It is important to get the brackets right, particularly when using Not statements.

Tip

To avoid any possibility of confusion, it is better to break up complex conditions into a series of related If statements.

The Else statement

The conditional statements can provide alternatives for when the condition is false, by including an **Else** statement, as follows:

```
if condition then
    begin
        truestatements;
    end
else
    begin
        falsestatements;
    end;
```

If the *condition* is true, the *truestatements* are executed; otherwise, the *falsestatements* are performed. The statement before Else must not have a semi-colon as If...Then...Else is treated as a single statement. Begin and End are not needed when there is only one statement:

```
if LeapYearInd = True then
    DaysInFeb := 29
else
    DaysInFeb := 28;
```

Using Else, only one of the alternatives will ever be executed.

Nested Ifs

For complex conditions you can **nest** the If statements. For instance:

```
if (NumMonth >= 1) and (NumMonth <= 12) then
    begin
        EditDays.Text := IntToStr(DaysInMonth);
        if (NumMonth = 2) and (LeapYearInd = True) then
            EditDays.Text := '29';
    end
else
    EditDays.Text := 'ERROR';
```

This illustrates the importance of indenting within If statements.

Case statements

When you are choosing between a number of alternatives, the **Case** statement is more appropriate than If. The structure for a Case statement is as follows:

```
case expression of
    test1: statement1;
    test2: statement2;
    ...;
else
    statementN;
end;
```

Take note

The Else section is not essential, but it lets you mop up any missing values. The End statement must always be included.

The *expression* (which must be an integer) is evaluated and the result is compared against the various test values. If the expression evaluates to *test1*, then *statement1* is executed; if it is *test2*, *statement2* is executed; and so on. If none of the tests matches the expression, the final statement (*statementN*) is executed. Unlike If statements, the statement before Else must have a semi-colon and the final statement is followed by End. Any of the statements can be replaced by multiple statements bracketed in Begin...End.

The tests for each case can be any of the following:

● A number (e.g. 7)

● A numeric expression (e.g. Sqr(A))

● A range of values (e.g. 2..6)

You can also combine any of these, separating them with commas; for example:

```
3, 6...8, Sqr(A): statement ;
```

Here, the corresponding code is executed if the expression evaluates to 3, 6, 7, 8 or the square of the variable A. The expression and the tests must all be integers.

An example is given below.

```pascal
function Nm(Txt: string): Integer;
var
    Txt1, Txt2: Char;
begin
    {Get first two chars of string}
    Txt1 := Txt[1];
    Txt2 := Txt[2];
    {Convert to 4-digit number}
    Nm := Ord(Txt1) * 100 + Ord(Txt2);
end;

procedure ProcessTaxCode(TaxCode: string;
                                    var TaxType: string);
var
    TaxCodeN: Integer;
begin
    {Convert first 2 chars of tax code to 4-digit number}
    TaxCodeN := Nm(TaxCode);
    {Determine type from first 2 chars of tax code}
    case TaxCodeN of
        4848..5757 {'00'..'99'}  : TaxType := 'Standard rates';
        7048..7057 {'F0'..'F9'} : TaxType := 'Non-accumulating';
        7548..7557 {'K0'..'K9'} : TaxType := 'Taxable benefits';
         6682       {'BR'}        : TaxType := 'Basic rate';
        7084, 7873, 6500 {'FT', 'NI', 'A'}
                                 : TaxType := 'Special case';
        7884       {'NT'}        : TaxType := 'No tax';
    else
        TaxType := 'Invalid tax code';
    end;
end;
```

Loops

The conditional statements give you the opportunity to decide whether or not some piece of code is to be executed but this still restricts you to a linear flow down through a procedure, from top to bottom. Sometimes you need to repeat a set of statements. Delphi provides looping instructions for three situations:

- Repeating a section of code a number of times

- Repeating while a condition is true

- Repeating until a condition becomes true

Each of these alternatives has its own set of Delphi instructions.

For loops

The simplest approach to looping is to repeat a group of statements a given number of times. This is achieved with the **For...To...Do** statement, which has the following structure:

```
for variable := start to end do
    begin
        statements;
    end;
```

The loop begins with the *variable* (which must be numeric) set to the *start* value and the *statements* are executed. The variable is then increased by 1. If the variable is greater than the *end* value, the loop ends and execution continues with the next statement in the procedure. Otherwise, the *statements* are executed again. This continues until the *end* value is exceeded.

If the *end* value is less than the *start* value when the loop is first entered (in a For...To...Do loop), the *statements* will never be executed.

The 'to' may be replaced by 'downto', reducing the variable value each time: in this case, the *end* should be less than the *start*.

The Begin and End statements may be omitted if only a single statement is to be executed in each loop.

For example:

```
for Country := 1 to 15 do
    ListEurope.Items.Add(StateName[Country]);
```

This loop is repeated 15 times, with each value of Country from 1 to 15. In each loop, the corresponding string from the array of country names is added to the list box.

You can **nest** one loop within another.

The following example uses a string grid (from the 'Additional' components) to display a calendar. Two separate loops are used to fill in the day names and change the width of alternate columns. A third loop for each column has another loop nested within it for each row. The inner loop is executed 35 times. The grid has the following properties:

Name: GridDay; ColCount: 13; RowCount: 7; Height: 178;

Width: 561; ScrollBars: ssNone

See overleaf for program

```
var
    Weekdays: array [1..7] of string;

procedure TCalendarForm.FormCreate(Sender: TObject);
var
    Row, Col: Integer;
    DayNum: Integer;
begin
    Weekdays[1] := 'Monday';      {Set up array of weekdays}
    Weekdays[2] := 'Tuesday';
    Weekdays[3] := 'Wednesday';
    Weekdays[4] := 'Thursday';
    Weekdays[5] := 'Friday';
    Weekdays[6] := 'Saturday';
    Weekdays[7] := 'Sunday';
    for Row := 0 to 6 do       {Fill in day names}
        GridDay.Cells[0, Row] := Weekdays[Row + 1];
    for Col := 1 to 11 do     {Reduce size of alternate cells}
        if Col in [1, 3, 5, 7, 9, 11] then
            GridDay.ColWidths[Col] := 16;
    DayNum := 1;
    for Col := 1 to 11 do  {Fill in day numbers}
        if Col in [1, 3, 5, 7, 9, 11] then
            for Row := 0 to 6 do
                begin
                  if DayNum <= 31 then
                    begin
                        GridDay.Cells[Col, Row] := IntToStr(DayNum);
                        DayNum := DayNum + 1;
                    end;
                end;
end;
```

The Cells property determines the contents of a particular cell. The ColWidths property sets the width of a particular cell.

128

Repeat and While

The **Repeat** and **While** statements are alternatives to For...To...Do loops and repeat the loop depending on whether some condition is true or false.

The Repeat loop has the following structure:

```
repeat
      statements;
until  condition;
```

There may be multiple *statements* in the loop, without Begin and End statements. The *condition* is tested at the end of the loop and, if it is false, the loop is repeated. The loop statements are therefore executed at least once, even if the condition is true initially.

The While loop has the structure:

```
while condition do
    begin
        statements;
    end;
```

Here, the *condition* is tested at the start of the loop; if it is true, the loop is executed and then the condition is tested again. Therefore, if the condition is false initially the loop statements will never be executed.

Each of these is useful in particular circumstances depending on whether or not you want the loop to be executed at least once.

An Until statement can be converted into a While statement by putting Not in front of the condition: for example, While A > 0 is the same as Until (Not A > 0) or Until A <= 0.

If you switch between Repeat and While loops remember that While needs Begin...End statements but Repeat does not (though you can do no harm by including them unnecessarily).

The program below demonstrates the use of these loops.

Address labels

```
procedure TAddressForm.ButtonProcessAddressClick
                                    (Sender: TObject);
var
    FullAddress: string;
    NextLine: string;
    LineNumber: Integer;
    CommaPos: Integer;
    HouseNumber: Boolean;
    HouseVal, ErrorCode: Integer;
    Address: array [1..10] of string;
const
    Comma = ',';
    CR = Chr(13) + Chr(10);    {Carriage return character}
begin
    {Takes full address from edit box and displays in memo,
     splitting lines at commas. Allows for address that starts
     with a house number}
    FullAddress := EditFullAddress.Text;    {Initialise variables}
    MemoAddress.Text := '';
    LineNumber := 1;
    HouseNumber := False;
    {Find first comma}
    CommaPos := Pos(Comma, FullAddress);
    {Loop while a comma has been found}
    while CommaPos > 0 do
        begin
            NextLine := Copy(FullAddress, 1, CommaPos - 1);
            if HouseNumber = True then
                begin
                    {Add next section to first line}
                    Address[1] := Address[1] + ', ' + NextLine;
                    HouseNumber := False;
```

> Indent the statements inside the loop to make it easier to see where the loop starts and ends.

> Indicator is set to True later in loop.

130

```
                end
            else
                {Put into next address line}
                Address[LineNumber] := NextLine;
            if (LineNumber = 1) and (Length(NextLine) < 5) then
                {First line starts with short word}
                begin
                    Val(NextLine, HouseVal, ErrorCode);
                    if HouseVal > 0 then
                        {Is a number, so add next part next time}
                        HouseNumber := True;
                end;
            {Advance line number if not a house number}
            if HouseNumber = False then
                LineNumber := LineNumber + 1;
            {Remove text that has been handled}
            Delete(FullAddress, 1, CommaPos);
            FullAddress := Trim(FullAddress);
            {Find next comma}
            CommaPos := Pos(Comma, FullAddress);
        end;  {end of while loop}
    {Put rest of address in array}
    Address[LineNumber] := FullAddress;
    {Fill memo with address}
    LineNumber := 1;      {Reset pointer}
    repeat
        MemoAddress.Text := MemoAddress.Text +
                            Address[LineNumber] + CR;
        LineNumber := LineNumber + 1;
    until Address[LineNumber] = '';
end;
```

> Could have used
> For i := 1 to LineNumber
> instead.

Exercises

1 Write a single procedure to add a given number of days, weeks, calendar months or years to a given date, returning the calculated date.

2 Write a function to check whether a password is valid. The function should return a value of True or False.

3 Write a program to display a calendar, as shown below. Use a string grid, from the 'Additional' components. The display should be updated whenever the month or year is changed.

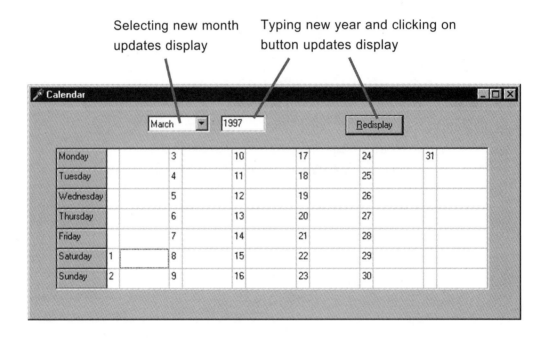

Selecting new month updates display

Typing new year and clicking on button updates display

For solutions to these exercises, see page 187.

7 Error handling

Debugging

When the program encounters a problem it cannot handle, it displays an error box.

When you click on the OK button, the code window is displayed with a coloured box around the line that has caused the problem. The program has not halted; it has only been temporarily suspended. Therefore, if the error is not too serious, you can make a correction and continue running.

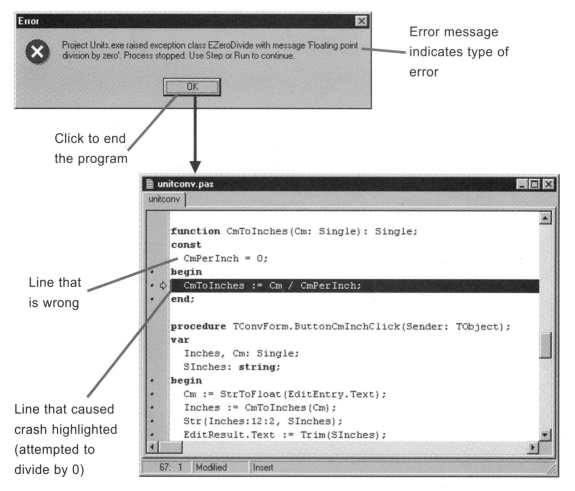

Error message indicates type of error

Click to end the program

Line that is wrong

Line that caused crash highlighted (attempted to divide by 0)

The error message itself is in the middle of the message box text. The program suggests that you continue running though you can of course halt altogether.

Several options are available:

- You can change the line that caused the problem and then press **[F9]** (Run I Run) to continue running the program.

- You can close down the program by selecting **[Ctrl-F2]** (Run I Program Reset).

- You can make more far-reaching changes to the program and then restart it by pressing **[Ctrl-F2]** and **[F9]** .

If you lose your place in the program, Run I Show Execution Point displays the procedure containing the next statement to be executed.

While the program is halted, you can also inspect the values of variables (see *Watching variables* on page 137).

Sometimes the changes you make are such that Delphi cannot continue running the program. A warning message is displayed and, if you click on OK, the changes are accepted and the program must then be restarted.

The other **debugging** options that are available when a program has been interrupted are described below.

Take note

When a program crashes, pressing [F9] restarts it at the line that caused the problem, not the following line.

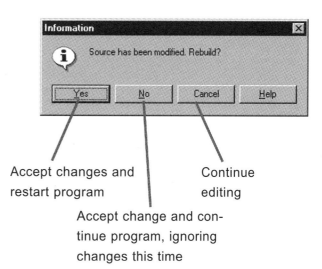

Accept changes and restart program

Accept change and continue program, ignoring changes this time

Continue editing

Breakpoints

You can force Delphi to halt execution at a particular point in the program by setting a **breakpoint**. Before running the program, put the cursor on the required line and select Run I Add Breakpoint. This gives you options for when the breakpoint is to become effective. Click on New. Alternatively, instead of using the menu option, click on the blue dot to the left of the line. The line is shown with a red background and a red circle is displayed in the grey area. When the program is run, it will halt at this point, before the line is executed.

Take note

You can also break into a program by selecting Run I Program Pause.

Having interrupted the program in this way, you can inspect the contents of variables, step through the code a line at a time, make minor changes to the code, or continue execution by pressing **[F9]**.

You can set several breakpoints at once; the program halts each time a breakpoint is encountered. A breakpoint is cancelled by clicking on the red circle to the left of the line.

Single-stepping

When a program halts because of an error or a breakpoint, the line that is about to be executed is highlighted. You can now run the program a line at a time using the following options:

● Press **[F7]** (Run I Trace Into) to execute the line; if the line contains a procedure or a function call, the procedure or function is displayed and you can continue to step through it a line at a time. This is called **single-stepping**.

● Press **[F8]** (Run I Step Over) to execute the line, including any procedure or function call; the next line in the current procedure is then highlighted.

● Move the cursor to some other point in the program and press **[F4]** (Run I Run To Cursor); execution continues until this point is reached.

When you have finished single-stepping, you can continue running with **[F9]** or stop with **[Ctrl-F2]**.

Watching variables

Having broken into a program, you can inspect the values of any variables or expressions. If you put the cursor on a variable name in the code, the current value pops up below the name.

You can also see how the value changes as the program progresses. Highlight a variable name or expression in the code and press **[Ctrl-C]** to copy it to the clipboard; then select Run | Add Watch (or press **[Ctrl-F5]**). Press **[Ctrl-V]** to paste the expression into the Watch Properties box, then click on OK. The Watch List window is displayed. This shows the expression and its current value. Each time you use Add Watch, another expression is added to the Watch List window. Now, as you single-step through the program, you will be able to see how the values of variables are affected by the code, making it much easier to identify the causes of problems.

Expression
to watch

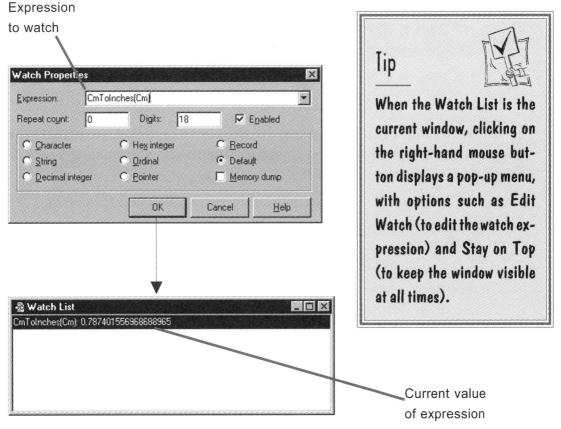

Current value
of expression

Tip

When the Watch List is the current window, clicking on the right-hand mouse button displays a pop-up menu, with options such as Edit Watch (to edit the watch expression) and Stay on Top (to keep the window visible at all times).

Trapping errors

You will have noticed that some of the programs you have been writing crash if an invalid entry is made (for instance, if an edit box that is supposed to contain a date is blank when a button is clicked). An error box is displayed, specifying the type of error (e.g. EZeroDivide or EConvertError); when you press **[F9]** to resume execution another, simpler message is displayed. If you run the EXE file from outside Delphi only the second 'user' message is displayed.

You can test for some errors – and correct them – using a control's Exit event. To be sure of handling all errors, however, you should include error-trapping statements in your code. These statements are activated when an error occurs.

System errors are referred to as **exceptions**; these occur when Delphi cannot process a statement for some reason. You can mark a block of statements for which specific exceptions are to be handled.

Error-trapping is implemented as follows:

1   Insert a **Try** statement in front of the block to be protected.

2   Insert an **Except** statement at the end of the block.

3   Follow the Except line with the statements that will correct the error (for instance, statements to display a warning message or change the contents of a variable).

4   End the error-handling statements with an End statement.

Now, if an error occurs when running within Delphi, only the first error message box is displayed; when running as a standalone program no error box is shown. After handling the error, execution continues after the Except block, so be careful not to include too many statements in the block. You can have several protected blocks in a procedure, and they may even be nested.

Most errors can be trapped, though only certain types of error are likely to occur in any procedure. You can check for the types of errors that may occur by testing for extreme values (zero, negative values, very large values, empty edit boxes, etc.) The error types are given in the detailed error box.

Error trapping

Sample procedure taken from Date Conversions program on pages 98-99.

```
procedure TDateForm.ButtonCalculateClick
                            (Sender: TObject);
{Amended to prevent program crashing if invalid date entered
 or edit box blank when Calculate button pressed}
var
    DateIn, ResultValue: TDateTime;
begin
    {Convert text date to date/time value}
    try
        DateIn := StrToDateTime(EditDateIn.Text);
    except
        on EConvertError do
            begin
                EditDateIn.Text := '01/01/97';
                DateIn := StrToDateTime('01/01/97');
            end;
    end;

    {After handling the error in the Except statement, the program
     continues here, not back in the protected block}

    {Convert to string and display}
    EditDTOut.Text := FloatToStr(DateIn);
    {Calculate weekday and display}
    EditDayOfWeek.Text := Weekdays[DayOfWeek(DateIn)];
    {Add/subtract number of days - must not be blank}
    ResultValue := DateIn + StrToInt(EditDaysIn.Text);
    EditResult.Text :=
            FormatDateTime('dd/mm/yyyy', ResultValue);
    {Update main heading}
    LabelNow.Caption := DateTimeToStr(Now);
end;
```

Add similar error-trapping for EditDaysIn edit box.

139

Exercises

1 Use the debugging options to interrupt the Contacts program when the Org Type is changed; watch the Dept value as it is changed.

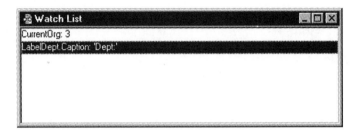

2 Add error-handling statements to the Calendar program so that it deals with a blank entry in the Year box.

For solutions to these exercises, see page 190.

8 Menus

The Menu Designer

Menus are added to forms using the MainMenu and PopupMenu components. MainMenu adds a drop-down menu bar to the form; PopupMenu adds a pop-up menu that appears when the user clicks the right-hand mouse button.

To create a drop-down menu, add a MainMenu component, in the same way as for any other component. The position of the component on the form is unimportant. There is no need to change the Name of the menu from MainMenu1.

The entries on the menu are set up using the **Menu Designer**, which is activated by double-clicking on the menu component. The first menu is shown as a blue box. The Object Inspector shows the properties for this menu.

MainMenu
component

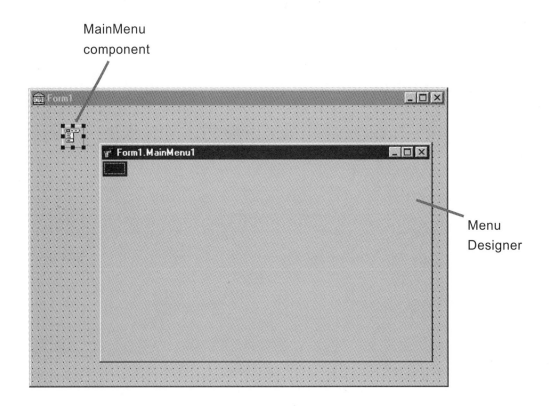

Menu
Designer

Caption and Name

Each menu or option is a separate object and therefore has its own Caption and Name. The Caption is the word or phrase that will appear in the drop-down menu; include an & in front of the character that is to be used as an **accelerator key** (e.g. &File for a menu that can be invoked by pressing [**Alt F**]). Traditionally, the Caption should end with three dots if the menu item leads to a dialogue box.

A useful convention is for the Name to consist of 'Menu' followed by the sequence of options (e.g. MenuFile for the File menu).

Adding options

When you have entered the first menu's Caption and Name, click below the menu name. A larger blue box appears, ready for the first option in the menu. Enter the Caption and Name, as for the menu (e.g. a Name of MenuFileNew for the File|New option, with a Caption of &New).

Add other options as needed.

To add a second menu, click on the grey box to the right of the first menu name, and continue as before.

Include & in front of accelerator key

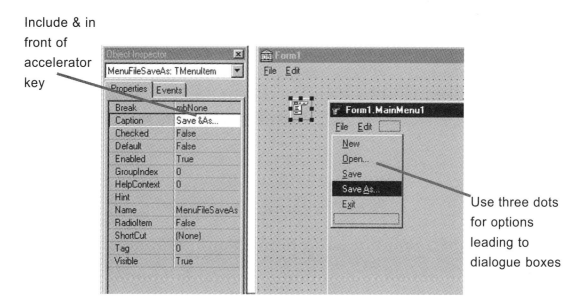

Use three dots for options leading to dialogue boxes

Editing the menus

Any of the menus or options can be edited later:

- Double-click on the menu component to show the Menu Designer.

- Click on a menu or option to display and edit its properties.

- Click on the grey box at the bottom of a menu or to the right of the last menu to add a new option or menu.

- Drag a menu item to a different position in the menu or into a different menu, to change the order of options.

- Drag an option onto the top line to promote it to a menu, or a menu onto another menu to demote it to an option.

- Click on a menu or option and press **[Del]** to delete it.

You can also use the normal cut and paste facilities to copy a menu component (including all its menus and options) to another form.

Sub-menus

As well as menus and options within menus, you can have sub-menus. These are created by pressing the right-hand mouse button and selecting Create Submenu. Alternatively, create the sub-menu as a menu and then drag it to the required position.

The sub-menu options can themselves become a further level of sub-menu by indenting the next set of items to a third level. However, you should not normally go beyond the first sub-menu.

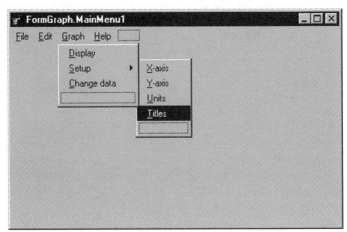

Menu properties

There are a number of properties that can be set or changed for each menu item. The Caption and Name are described above; the other properties are detailed here.

Boolean properties

The Object Inspector has four main Boolean properties:

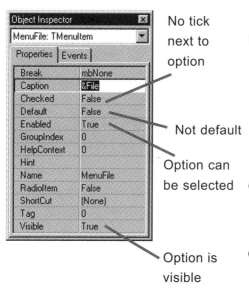

No tick
next to
option

Not default

Option can
be selected

Option is
visible

- The **Checked** property, when True, places a tick on the left of the menu option.

- The **Default** property, when True, makes the item the default option for the menu; when the menu name is double-clicked, the default option is activated. There can be only one default option per menu, and menu names cannot have Default set to True.

- The **Enabled** property, when False, greys out the menu or option; clicking on the menu or option has no effect.

- The **Visible** property, when False, hides the option when the menu is displayed (or hides the menu).

Usually, you will want to leave the properties as they are when developing the menu system but change them while the program is running. For instance, an option may be used for switching some feature of the program on or off. Clicking on the option will set Checked to True (and place a tick against it); clicking on it again will set Checked to False (and remove the tick). As another example, after saving a file the File I Save option may have its Enabled property set to False; as soon as further changes are made to the data the Enabled property can be set to True again. The Visible property can be used for restricting options: for instance, some menu options may be visible only to users with certain passwords.

Shortcut keys

You can attach a **shortcut key** to any item in the menu. This is a key combination that the user can press to activate the menu option without having to click on the option itself. For example, it is usual for the File|Save option to have a **[Ctrl-S]** shortcut, so that the save routine is invoked when the user presses **[Ctrl-S]**.

A shortcut is attached to an item by clicking on the Shortcut setting and then selecting from the drop-down list. When you run the program and display the menu, the shortcut is shown to the right of the option name.

Separator bars

For long menus, it is useful to split the options into groups. This is done by inserting a **separator bar**. The bar is included as an item in the menu with a special caption of '–'. The separator bar should also be given a Name (which will be needed if, for example, you want to make the bar invisible from within the program).

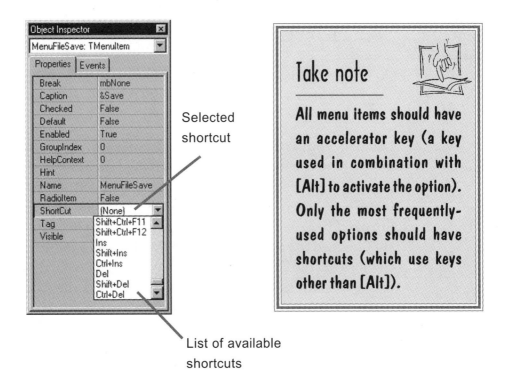

Selected shortcut

List of available shortcuts

Take note

All menu items should have an accelerator key (a key used in combination with [Alt] to activate the option). Only the most frequently-used options should have shortcuts (which use keys other than [Alt]).

Option groups

A group of options in a menu can be made to act like a group of radio buttons. The options must be given the same GroupIndex setting (a number other than 0) and all must have RadioItem set to True. One option will have a radio button placed next to it. When the user clicks on a different option, the radio buton will move to that option.

Other properties

Four other properties may be useful in more complex applications:

● **Break** lets you split a menu into columns.

● **HelpContext** provides a link to a help file.

● **Hint** displays a hint box when the cursor is placed over the option.

● **Tag** stores additional user-defined information.

Hint and Tag are also properties for all other components. For more information on these properties, see the Delphi on-line help.

Take note

The properties for the Popup Menu are identical to those of the Main Menu. In this case, the menu only appears when the user clicks the right-hand mouse button. Only a single menu is allowed but items in this menu can lead to sub-menus(in the Menu Designer, select the menu item, click the right-hand mouse button and select Create Submenu).

In order to activate the Popup Menu, you must select its name in the form's PopupMenu property. (By default, the form's Menu property is set to MainMenu1.)

Menu events

Menu items respond to an OnClick event, which is activated either by clicking on the menu option or by pressing the accelerator key or shortcut.

For menus and sub-menus, the OnClick event results in the list of options dropping down (but may also have a Click procedure attached). For menu options, you need to supply an OnClick procedure. The code for this is added by double-clicking on the option in the Menu Designer.

Tip

Some menu options will duplicate the effect of other events. For instance, selecting the File | Exit option will be the same as clicking on the Exit button. In such cases, the menu option's OnClick event should call the procedure for the corresponding event (e.g. MenuFileExitClick should call ButtonExitClick).

The Edit menu

Most applications have an Edit menu with the following options:

Cut   Deletes highlighted text and copies to clipboard

Copy   Copies highlighted text to clipboard

Paste   Pastes text from clipboard at cursor position (replacing any highlighted text)

Clear   Deletes highlighted text

The **clipboard** is an object that is supplied with every Windows application. It does not have any physical appearance or events but it does have some useful methods and properties. Most useful is the AsText property, which contains up to 255 characters of text. To access the clipboard, you must add **Clipbrd** to the Uses statement.

The clipboard can be used in conjunction with the following edit box and memo properties:

SelText String of highlighted characters (blank if none selected)

SelLength Length of highlighted string

SelStart Current cursor position (0 if in front of first character)

The procedures below show how the Edit menu can be implemented.

Edit menu

```
procedure TForm1.MenuEditCutClick(Sender: TObject);
begin    {Assumes text is in edit box Edit1}
    Clipboard.Clear;              {Clear the clipboard}
    Clipboard.AsText := Edit1.SelText; {Copy highlighted
                             text to clipboard}
    Edit1.SelText := '';          {Delete highlighted text}
end;

procedure TForm1.MenuEditCopyClick(Sender: TObject);
begin
    Clipboard.Clear;              {Clear the clipboard}
    Clipboard.AsText := Edit1.SelText; {Copy text to clipboard}
end;

procedure TForm1.MenuEditPasteClick(Sender: TObject);
begin {Replace highlighted text with contents of clipboard}
    Edit1.SelText := Clipboard.AsText;
end;

procedure TForm1.MenuEditClearClick(Sender: TObject);
begin   {Add warning message here if needed}
    Edit1.Text := ''        {Delete all text}
end;
```

> For more than 255 characters you must create a text buffer – see TClipboard in Delphi help.

Exercises

1   Add the following menu options to the Contacts program's front-end window:

Menu/option	Access key	Shortcut	Effect when clicked
File	f		(Menu)
Open...	o	Ctrl + O	(Leave empty)
Save...	s	Ctrl + S	(Leave empty)
Exit	x		Ends program
Window	w		(Menu)
Contacts...	c		Displays Details screen
Calls...	l		Displays Calls screen
Close All	a		Closes all other windows
Help	h		(Menu)
About...	a		Displays information box

Create appropriate Click procedures for these options.

2   Add the following menu options to the Details window:

Menu/Option	Access key	Shortcut	Effect when clicked
File	f		(Menu)
Save...	s	Ctrl + S	(Leave empty)
Abandon	a		Same effect as Cancel
Exit	x		Same effect as OK

Create appropriate Click procedures for these options.

3   Add the following menu options to the Calls window:

Menu/Option	Access key	Shortcut	Effect when clicked
File	f		(Menu)
Save...	s	Ctrl + S	(Leave empty)
Abandon	a		Same effect as Cancel
Exit	x		Same effect as OK
Edit	e		(Menu)
Cut	t	Ctrl + X	Cuts text to clipboard
Copy	c	Ctrl + C	Copies text to clipboard
Paste	p	Ctrl + V	Paste text from clipboard
Clear	l		Deletes all text
			(asks for confirmation)

Create appropriate Click procedures for these options.

For solutions to these exercises, see page 191.

9 Files

File selection

Delphi provides a number of standard dialogue boxes for use in applications. These can be found in the 'Dialogs' group of components.

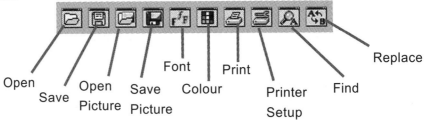

The Open and Save dialogue boxes are standard Windows 95 dialogue boxes for loading or saving files. These dialogue boxes are activated with the **Execute** method. For example:

        SaveDialog1.Execute;

The following properties are particularly useful:

- **InitialDir** sets the directory that is opened when the dialogue box is displayed.

- **Title** sets the title for the dialogue box (which defaults to 'Open' or 'Save As').

- **Filter** allows you to list the file types that may be displayed. An editor is displayed in which you can specify the Filter Name and Filter (e.g. 'Text files (*.txt)' and '*.txt').

- **FilterIndex** specifies the default Filter (usually 1, for the first filter in the list).

- **Options** sets a wide range of options for the box: for instance, to stipulate that any filename entered must already exist.

- **FileName** holds the name of the file last selected, including full directory path.

Examples of procedures that use these dialogue boxes are given below.

Open and Save

```
procedure TFilesForm.ButtonOpenClick(Sender: TObject);
var
    FName: string;
begin            {Selects file and displays name}
    with OpenDialog1 do
        begin
            Title := 'Open new text file';
            InitialDir := 'c:\reports';
            Filter := 'Text files (*.txt)|*.txt';
        end;
    OpenDialog1.Execute;
    FName := OpenDialog1.FileName;
    if FName > '' then EditFilename.Text := FName
    else EditFilename.Text := 'No file selected';
end;

procedure TFilesForm.ButtonSaveClick(Sender: TObject);
var
    FName: string;
begin
    with SaveDialog1 do
        begin
            Title := 'Save text file';
            InitialDir := 'c:\reports';
            Filter := 'Text files (*.txt)|*.txt';
            FileName := '';
        end;
    SaveDialog1.Execute;
    FName := SaveDialog1.FileName;
    if FName > '' then LabelStatus.Caption := 'Saved'
    else LabelStatus.Caption := 'Save data';
end;
```

See dialogue box on page 154.

'If' statements have been compressed to save space.

The With...Do statement allows you to omit a component name from property declarations.

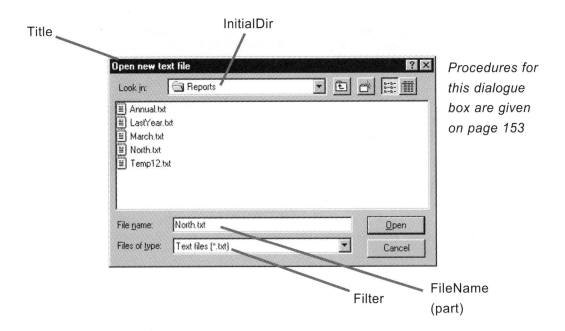

Title

InitialDir

Procedures for
this dialogue
box are given
on page 153

Filter

FileName
(part)

Common dialogue boxes

The other common dialogue boxes provide a simple way to perform standard Windows operations:

- **OpenPictureDialog** lets you open a picture file, with a preview box; **SavePictureDialog** saves a picture file.

- **FontDialog** displays a standard font selection box.

- **ColorDialog** leads to a colour selection box, including the ability to define custom colours.

- **PrintDialog** provides access to the Windows printer dialogue box, including the usual Properties box; **PrinterSetupDialog** adds options to choose paper size etc.

- **FindDialog** gives the user the ability to search for text; **ReplaceDialog** lets you replace this with new text.

The properties vary for these components and can be viewed on-line by searching help for the component class (for instance, search for TFindDialog for the Find dialogue box).

File operations

Within a program, you may want to delete, rename or copy a file, or carry out directory operations. Delphi provides a means of handling all these tasks.

- The **DeleteFile** statement deletes a file:

    result := DeleteFile(*filespec*);

  The *filespec* is a string containing the name of the file to be deleted, including directory path. If no path is given, the current directory is assumed. The *result* is a variable which contains a value of True if the operation was successful or False if it was not.

- The **RenameFile** statement renames a file:

    result := RenameFile(*oldname, newname*);

  The *oldname* is a string containing the original path and name; *newname* is the file's new name. If the new name contains a different path, the file will be moved to that directory.

- The **CopyFile** statement copies a file:

    result := CopyFile(*source, destination, replace*);

  The *source* is a string containing the name of the file to be copied. The *destination* is the name of the new file. If the *replace* value is False, the source file is copied even if the destination file already exists; if *replace* is True, the copy is made only if the destination does not exist. Note that both filenames are null-terminated strings (see example on page 158 for how to handle such strings).

In each case, you can only work with one file at a time and the current drive and directory are assumed unless otherwise specified.

Three built-in procedures, **MkDir**, **RmDir** and **ChDir**, create, delete and change directories respectively. Each must be followed by a string containing the directory name in brackets.

The program below uses three components from the 'Win 3.1' group (DriveComboBox, DialogListBox and FileListBox) to display the contents of a directory and perform housekeeping operations.

The dialogue box illustrated on page 158 uses these procedures.

```
implementation

{$R *.DFM}

{Error-handling statements have been omitted to save space}

procedure THousekeepForm.DriveComboBox1Change
                              (Sender: TObject);
begin
    DirectoryListBox1.Drive := DriveComboBox1.Drive;
    FileListBox1.Drive := DriveComboBox1.Drive;
end;

procedure THousekeepForm.DirectoryListBox1Change
                              (Sender: TObject);
begin
    FileListBox1.Directory := DirectoryListBox1.Directory;
end;

procedure THousekeepForm.FileListBox1Change
                              (Sender: TObject);
begin
    EditOldname.Text := FileListBox1.Filename;
end;

procedure CheckResult(result:  Boolean);
begin
    {If operation was not successful display error message}
    if result = False then
        MessageDlg('Operation Failed', mtError, [mbOK], 0);
    {Update the display}
    HousekeepForm.FileListBox1.Update;
    HousekeepForm.EditNewname.Text := '';
end;
```

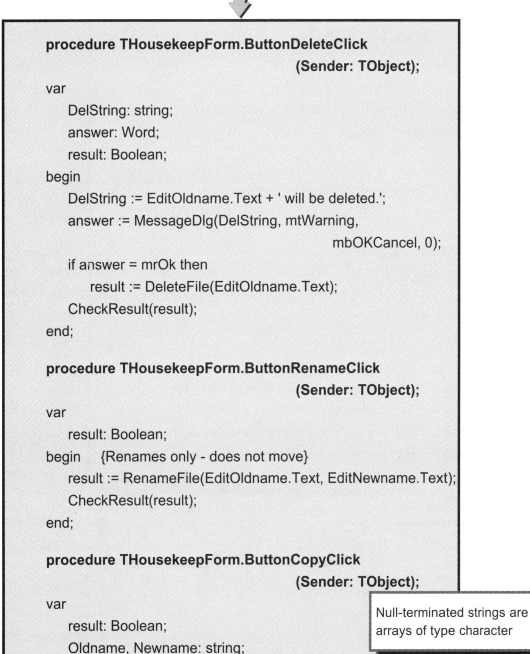

```
    procedure THousekeepForm.ButtonDeleteClick
                                    (Sender: TObject);
var
    DelString: string;
    answer: Word;
    result: Boolean;
begin
    DelString := EditOldname.Text + ' will be deleted.';
    answer := MessageDlg(DelString, mtWarning,
                                    mbOKCancel, 0);
    if answer = mrOk then
        result := DeleteFile(EditOldname.Text);
    CheckResult(result);
end;

    procedure THousekeepForm.ButtonRenameClick
                                    (Sender: TObject);
var
    result: Boolean;
begin    {Renames only - does not move}
    result := RenameFile(EditOldname.Text, EditNewname.Text);
    CheckResult(result);
end;

    procedure THousekeepForm.ButtonCopyClick
                                    (Sender: TObject);
var
    result: Boolean;
    Oldname, Newname: string;
    POldname, PNewname: array [0..127] of Char;
begin
    Oldname := EditOldname.Text;
```

Null-terminated strings are arrays of type character

StrPCopy cretes a null-terminated string from an ordinary string.

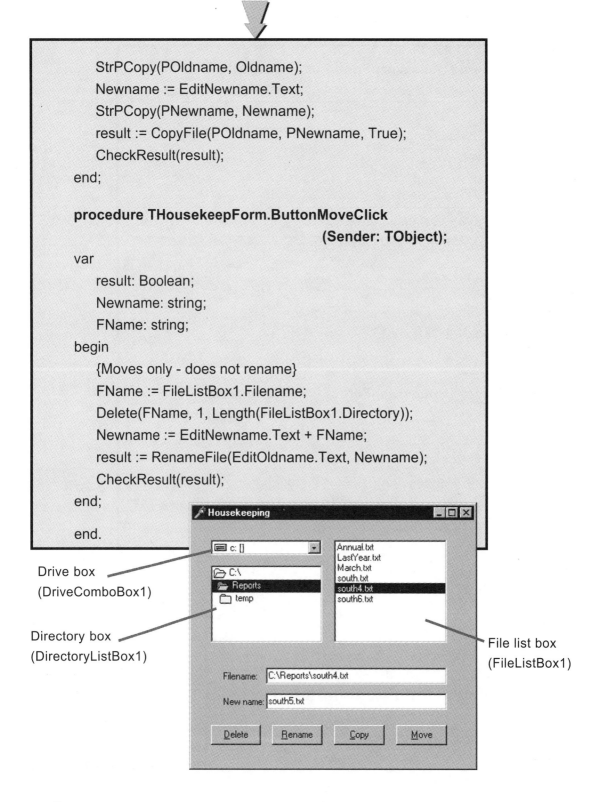

```
        StrPCopy(POldname, Oldname);
        Newname := EditNewname.Text;
        StrPCopy(PNewname, Newname);
        result := CopyFile(POldname, PNewname, True);
        CheckResult(result);
    end;

procedure THousekeepForm.ButtonMoveClick
                                (Sender: TObject);

var
    result: Boolean;
    Newname: string;
    FName: string;
begin
    {Moves only - does not rename}
    FName := FileListBox1.Filename;
    Delete(FName, 1, Length(FileListBox1.Directory));
    Newname := EditNewname.Text + FName;
    result := RenameFile(EditOldname.Text, Newname);
    CheckResult(result);
    end;

    end.
```

Drive box
(DriveComboBox1)

Directory box
(DirectoryListBox1)

File list box
(FileListBox1)

Housekeeping

c: []

C:\
Reports
temp

Annual.txt
LastYear.txt
March.txt
south.txt
south4.txt
south6.txt

Filename: C:\Reports\south4.txt

New name: south5.txt

Delete   Rename   Copy   Move

Sequential files

Sequential files consist of a series of lines of text, and are often referred to as **ASCII files**. Each line of text is terminated by a carriage-return character (ASCII 13) and the file ends with Ctrl-Z (ASCII 26). Although ASCII files can include extended ASCII characters, they are usually restricted to the standard characters, in the range 32 to 126. Sequential files are stored with one byte for each character and can be viewed, edited or created by Notepad.

Delphi provides a group of instructions for handling sequential files. At their simplest, sequential files are written or read one complete line at a time (a line consisting of everything up to the next carriage-return character). Therefore, they are suitable for storing text: for example, the output from a multi-line text box.

Sequential files can also be saved in the **comma-delimited** format. In these files, each line consists of one or more data values, separated by commas. Text items should be enclosed in double quotes. When a line of data is read from a sequential file, each value is assigned to a variable.

Text file (ASCII file)

```
First contact December, 1994
Originally with WWS
Joined ARV January, 1996
```

Comma-delimited file

```
"Jim Smith", 1023, "Sales", 20, "South"
"Jo Edwards", 1036, "Sales", 20, "East"
"Ellen Howe", 1045, "Support", 12, "South"
```

Take note

You cannot both read and write to a sequential file at the same time.

Take note

Text in comma-delimited files does not have to be enclosed in quotes but it is less confusing if it is. If the text contains a comma, double quotes *must* be used.

Creating sequential files

There are three stages in creating a sequential file: opening the file, writing the data and closing the file.

Before opening the file, a **filevariable** must be declared:

```
var
    filevar : textfile;
```

A filename (including directory path) must be associated with the file variable:

```
AssignFile(filevar, filespec);
```

The file is then **opened** with one of the following statementas:

```
Rewrite(filevar);      {create new file}

Append(filevar);      {open existing file, add new text}
```

If you use **Rewrite**, a new file is created and any existing file with the same name is deleted. If you use **Append**, the new data is added to the end of the existing file (or a new file is created, if one does not yet exist).

Data is written to a sequential file with the **Write** statement. Each statement should write one line of data to the file and be terminated by a carriage return. The format of these statements is as follows:

```
Write(filevar, value1, value2, ...);
```

To write comma-delimited files, you must place any text values in double quotes (ASCII character 34) and write a comma between values, with a CR/LF sequence at the end. Otherwise, any values you write appear as a single string of text.

The file is **closed** with a statement in the form:

```
CloseFile(filevar);
```

The CloseFile statement is essential, as it stores away any unwritten data held in memory.

Reading sequential files

Corresponding to the creation of a sequential file, there are three stages for reading such a file: opening the file, reading the data and closing the file.

The file is **opened** with the following statements:

```
AssignFile(filevar, filespec);
Reset(filevar);
```

Data is read from the file with this statement:

```
ReadLn(filevar, string);
```

The statement reads an entire line into a *string*. If the text is from a comma-delimited file it must be unpacked into separate variables.

The **CloseFile** statement is the same as before.

Sequential files must always be read from the beginning of the file. You can use the **eof** function to detect the end of the file. (The function returns a True value when the end-of-file marker has been reached.) The function takes the file variable as its argument.

The following procedures demonstrate how File | Open and File | Save commands can read and write data from the Calendar program.

Calendar files — 1

```
procedure ClearCalendar;
var
    Row, Col: Integer;
begin
    for Col := 2 to 12 do
        if Col in [2, 4, 6, 8, 10, 12] then
            for Row := 0 to 6 do
                CalendarForm.GridDay.Cells[Col, Row] := '';
end;

{Add to end of TCalendarForm.FormCreate
 and to end of TCalendarForm.ButtonRedisplayClick}
    ClearCalendar;                    {Clear calendar}
    MenuFileOpenClick(Sender);      {Read in existing data}
```

Additions to Calendar program from page 132.

161

```
procedure MakeFilename(var CalendarFile: string);
var
    SCurrentYear, SCurrentMonth: string;
const
    CalendarDir = 'c:\calendar\';   {Assume directory exists}
begin
    SCurrentMonth := Copy(CalendarForm.ComboMonth.Text, 1, 3);
    SCurrentYear := Trim(CalendarForm.EditYear.Text);
    CalendarFile := CalendarDir + SCurrentMonth
                                        + SCurrentYear + '.txt';
end;

procedure TCalendarForm.MenuFileSaveClick(Sender: TObject);
var
    CalendarFile: string;
    CalFile: textfile;
    Row, Col: Integer;
    SRow, SCol: string;
    DayNo, DayText, DayNoQ: string;
const
    CR = Chr(13) + Chr(10);
    Comma = ',';
    Quotes = Chr(34);
begin    {Saves calendar when user presses [Ctrl-S]}
    MakeFilename(CalendarFile);
    AssignFile(CalFile, CalendarFile);
    Rewrite(CalFile);
    for Col := 2 to 12 do
        if Col in [2, 4, 6, 8, 10, 12] then
            begin
                for Row := 0 to 6 do
                    begin
                        DayNo := GridDay.Cells[Col - 1, Row];
                        if DayNo > '0' then
                            begin
                                SCol := Quotes + IntToStr(Col) + Quotes;
                                SRow := Quotes + IntToStr(Row) + Quotes;
                                DayNoQ := Quotes + DayNo + Quotes;
                                DayText := Quotes +
                                        GridDay.Cells[Col, Row] + Quotes;
                                Write(CalFile, SCol, Comma, SRow, Comma,
                                        DayNoQ, Comma, DayText, CR);
                            end;
                    end;
            end;
    CloseFile(CalFile)
end;
```

You can check the contents of the file using Notepad.

```
procedure GetString(var InputText, FirstString: string);
const
    Comma = ',';
begin
    {Get first string, omitting quotes and comma}
    FirstString := Copy(InputText, 2, Pos(Comma, InputText) - 3);
    Delete(InputText, 1, Pos(Comma, InputText));
end;

procedure TCalendarForm.MenuFileOpenClick(Sender: TObject);
var
    CalendarFile: string;
    CalFile: textfile;
    Row, Col: Integer;
    SRow, SCol: string;
    DayText, DayNoQ: string;
    InputText: string;
begin
    ClearCalendar;
    {Open existing calendar file if it exists}
    MakeFilename(CalendarFile);
    AssignFile(CalFile, CalendarFile);
    {Error checking for file errors}
    try
        Reset(CalFile);
         while not eof(CalFile) do
            begin
                ReadLn(CalFile, InputText);
                {Split input line into strings}
                if InputText > '' then
                    begin
                        GetString(InputText, SCol);
                        GetString(InputText, SRow);
                        GetString(InputText, DayNoQ);
                        DayText := Copy(InputText, 2,
                                            Length(InputText) - 2);
                        Col := StrToInt(SCol);
                        Row := StrToInt(SRow);
                        GridDay.Cells[Col, Row] := DayText;
                    end;
            end;
        CloseFile(CalFile)
    except
        {Ignore errors but handle to omit error message}
        on EInOutError do {do nothing};
    end;
end;
```

Random access files

Random access files store data in a record-based format. The file consists of a number of records, each of which has the same size and layout. The advantage over sequential files is that you can read and write records in any order; records are accessed by specifying a record number. However, random access files are not suitable for variable-length data.

Record structure

You must define the structure of the records before attempting to read or write them. This is done with a **Type** declaration, as follows:

```
type
    recordtype =
        record
            variable1: type;
            variable2: type;

            ...
        end;
    filetype = file of recordtype;
```

The final statement defines a file type as being made up of records of the specified record type. Any string variables must be given an explicit length by declaring them as follows:

```
variable : string[length];
```

'Type' is usually included after the Implementation statement.

Accessing records

Records are read or written in three stages: opening the file; reading or writing the data; and closing the file.

To access the file, use file and record variables, declared as follows:

```
var
    filevar : filetype;
    recordvar : recordtype;
```

The file is opened with AssignFile and either Rewrite (for new files) or Reset (for existing files), as before. Once open, files can be both read and written.

To write records, you must first fill a record by assigning values to the individual variables, using statements in the format:

> *recordvar.variable* := *expression;*

For a number of such assignments, use the With...Do statement.

> with *recordvar* do
>   begin
>   *variable1* := *expression1*;
>   *variable2* := *expression2*;
>   ...
>   end;

Tip

The number of records in a random access file is given by FileSize(filevar) and is one greater than the final record number.

A completed record is located and written with the following statements:

> Seek(*filevar, recordnumber*);
> Write(*filevar, recordvar*);

The *recordnumber* starts at 0 for the first record. If the number is beyond the current end-of-file, the file is extended. (Unused records will contain rubbish unless specifically cleared.) After writing a record, the program points to the next record, so a Seek statement is not needed when writing a series of consecutive records.

Data is read from the file using a **Read** statement, as follows:

> Seek(*filevar, recordnumber*);   {if necessary}
> Read(*filevar, recordvar*);

The individual variables in the *recordvar* are filled with the corresponding data from the record and can be unpacked into normal variables.

The procedures below provide alternative File operations for the Calendar program, this time storing the data in a random access file.

```
{Insert at start of Implementation section}
type
    CalRecordType =
        record
            RowNum: Integer;
            ColNum: Integer;
            DayString: string[30];
        end;
    CalFileType = file of CalRecordType;

procedure ClearCalendar;
{New procedure as for page 162}

procedure TCalendarForm.FormCreate(Sender: TObject);
procedure TCalendarForm.ButtonRedisplayClick(Sender:TObject);
{Changes to two procedures as for page 162}

{Replacement procedures}
procedure MakeFilename(var CalendarFile: string);
var
    SCurrentYear, SCurrentMonth: string;
const
    CalendarDir = 'c:\calendar\';   {Assume directory exists}
begin
    SCurrentMonth := Copy(CalendarForm.ComboMonth.Text, 1, 3);
    SCurrentYear := Trim(CalendarForm.EditYear.Text);
    CalendarFile := CalendarDir + SCurrentMonth + SCurrentYear
                                                        + '.dat';
end;

procedure TCalendarForm.MenuFileSaveClick(Sender: TObject);
var
    CalendarFile: string;
    CalFile: CalFileType;
    Row, Col: Integer;
    DayRec: CalRecordType;
    CellNum: Integer;
begin
    {Saves calendar when user presses [Ctrl-S]}
    MakeFilename(CalendarFile);
    AssignFile(CalFile, CalendarFile);
    Rewrite(CalFile);
    CellNum := 0;
    for Col := 2 to 12 do
        if Col in [2, 4, 6, 8, 10, 12] then
            begin
                for Row := 0 to 6 do
```

166

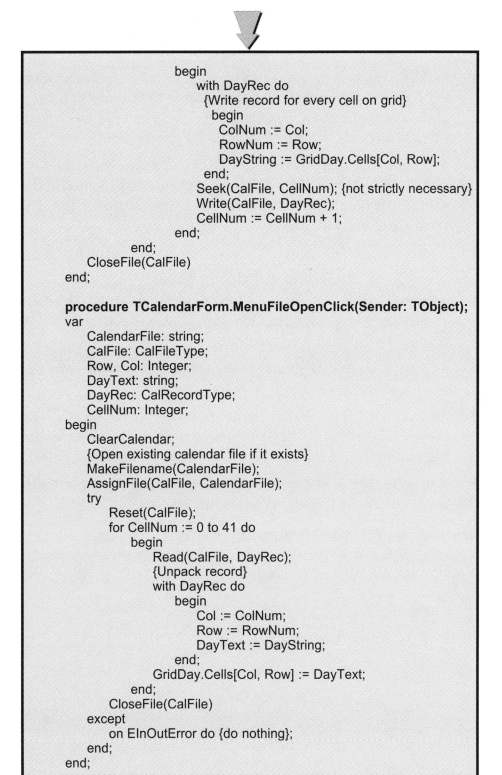

```
                    begin
                        with DayRec do
                            {Write record for every cell on grid}
                               begin
                                 ColNum := Col;
                                 RowNum := Row;
                                 DayString := GridDay.Cells[Col, Row];
                               end;
                            Seek(CalFile, CellNum); {not strictly necessary}
                            Write(CalFile, DayRec);
                            CellNum := CellNum + 1;
                        end;
                end;
         CloseFile(CalFile)
   end;

   procedure TCalendarForm.MenuFileOpenClick(Sender: TObject);
   var
       CalendarFile: string;
       CalFile: CalFileType;
       Row, Col: Integer;
       DayText: string;
       DayRec: CalRecordType;
       CellNum: Integer;
   begin
       ClearCalendar;
       {Open existing calendar file if it exists}
       MakeFilename(CalendarFile);
       AssignFile(CalFile, CalendarFile);
       try
           Reset(CalFile);
           for CellNum := 0 to 41 do
               begin
                   Read(CalFile, DayRec);
                   {Unpack record}
                   with DayRec do
                       begin
                           Col := ColNum;
                           Row := RowNum;
                           DayText := DayString;
                       end;
                   GridDay.Cells[Col, Row] := DayText;
               end;
           CloseFile(CalFile)
       except
           on EInOutError do {do nothing};
       end;
   end;
```

Exercises

1   In the Contacts program, add a combo box to the front-end form to hold a list of contacts. Allow new names to be typed at the top of the combo box. Add a command button which, when clicked, will add any new name to the list in the combo box.

2   Add code to the File I Save option to create a sequential file with a CON extension (using a standard dialogue box to choose the name). The file should contain the list of contacts, associating a record number with each one.

3   Add code for File I Open to fill the combo box from the list in the file. Store the filename in a label on the form.

4   Add code for the File I Save option on the Calls screen. The calls should be stored in a text file with a filename based on the contact's position in the combo box.

5   Add code so that the current contact's calls (if any) are displayed when the Calls screen is loaded.

6   Add code for the File I Save option on the Details screen. The contact's details should be stored as a single record in a file with the same name as the contacts list file but an extension of DTL.

7   Add code so that the current contact's details (if any) are displayed when the Details screen is loaded.

For solutions to these exercises, see page 193.

10 Graphics

Pictures

 The **image** control (from the 'Additional' components) displays a bitmap file, icon file or Windows metafile. (These have extensions of BMP, ICO and WMF respectively.)

The **Picture** property can be set at design time and specifies the filename of the picture to be displayed. In that case, the picture file is incorporated into the form file (and hence in the executable file, making it considerably larger).

Alternatively, you can specify the filename at run time with the **LoadFromFile** method of the Picture property; the picture file is then held separately from the executable file (but must be supplied with the application). For example:

```
Image1.Picture.LoadFromFile('c:\logo.bmp');
```

In this case, a file called 'logo.bmp' in the root directory of drive C is loaded into the image box.

The **Height** and **Width** properties set the size of the image box; if the box is not large enough, the top left-hand corner of the picture is displayed.

The box expands to fit the picture if **AutoSize** is True. The **Stretch** property, if set to True, results in the image being stretched to fit the box.

The **Left** and **Top** properties determine the position of the picture on the form.

The **Visible** property can be set to False to hide the picture.

Using one or more pictures, you can create simple animations, as demonstrated by the procedure opposite. In this case, the animation is generated by changing the Left and Top properties of an image. When these properties change, Windows redraws the image. The result can be rather jerky but can be improved by changing the Step value and the timer interval.

Bounce

```
var
    {Variables for use throughout program}
    Horiz, Vert: Integer;   {1=Right/Down, -1=Left/Up}
    Step: Integer;

procedure TForm1.Button1Click(Sender: TObject);
begin
    {Animation begins when button is clicked}
    {Load image and set initial direction}
    Image1.Picture.LoadFromFile('c:\bounce.bmp');
    Horiz := 1;           {Start going right}
    Vert := 1;            {and down}
    Step := 5;
end;

procedure TForm1.Timer1Timer(Sender: TObject);
begin
    {Image is moved at each interval of timer}
    Image1.Left := Image1.Left + Horiz * Step;
    Image1.Top := Image1.Top + Vert * Step;
    {Check to see if at edge; if so, change direction}
    if Image1.Left + Image1.Width >=
                        Form1.ClientWidth - Step then
        Horiz := -1;
    if Image1.Left <= Step then
        Horiz := 1;
    if Image1.Top + Image1.Height >=
                        Form1.ClientHeight - Step then
        Vert := -1;
    if Image1.Top <= Step then
        Vert := 1;
end;
```

Shapes and lines

 The **Shape** component in the Additional group adds a rectangle or oval. The fill colour and pattern are set by the **Brush** property; the colour and style of the outline are determined by **Pen**. The **Shape** property lets you choose between a number of rectangles and ellipses.

Canvas methods

You can also draw on the surface of forms using the **Canvas**, which is a property of the form. This has its own set of methods for drawing lines and shapes and for displaying text.

For example, the **MoveTo** method moves the drawing position to a specific point and **LineTo** draws a line from the current point to another point. Points on the cavas are defined by a pair of (X,Y) co-ordinates. The X co-ordinate is the distance (in pixels) from the left of the form; the Y co-ordinate is measured from the top. For example:

```
procedure TForm1.Button1Click(Sender: TObject);
begin
    with Canvas do
        begin
          {Draw line across middle of window}
          MoveTo(0, ClientHeight div 2);
          LineTo(ClientWidth, ClientHeight div 2);
        end;
    end;
```

You can add shapes using methods such as **Ellipse** and **Rectangle**. The colour and pattern of the inside of the shapes is set by the canvas **Brush** property. **Polygon** draws a filled shape; **Polyline** draws a multi-sided, empty shape.

The **TextOut** method 'prints' text directly on the form or picture box. The font is changed with the **Font** property (for the canvas, not the form).

The program opposite demonstrates a very simple drawing program.

```
var DrawLine, Freehand, FreehandOn: Boolean;

procedure TForm1.ButtonLineClick(Sender: TObject);
begin     {Draw a line}
    DrawLine := True; Freehand := False; FreehandOn := False;
end;

procedure TForm1.ButtonFreeClick(Sender: TObject);
begin     {Draw freehand}
    DrawLine := False; Freehand := True; FreehandOn := False;
end;

procedure TForm1.FormMouseDown(Sender: TObject;
    Button: TMouseButton; Shift: TShiftState; X, Y: Integer);
begin     {Start drawing line - position from mouse parameters}
    if DrawLine = True then Canvas.MoveTo(X, Y);
end;

procedure TForm1.FormMouseUp(Sender: TObject; ...
begin        {Stop drawing line}
    if DrawLine = True then Canvas.LineTo(X, Y);
end;

procedure TForm1.FormClick(Sender: TObject);
begin        {Click to switch on or off}
    if Freehand = True then FreehandOn := not(FreehandOn);
end;

procedure TForm1.FormMouseMove(Sender: TObject; ...
begin
    if Freehand = True then        {If not freehand, do nothing}
        if FreehandOn = True then Canvas.LineTo(X, Y)
        else Canvas.MoveTo(X, Y);
end;
```

Printing

The contents of a form can be printed to the standard Windows printer using the **Print** method.

For example, the following procedure can be added to the Calendar program to print the calendar for a month.

```
procedure TCalendarForm.ButtonPrintClick(Sender: TObject);
begin
    CalendarForm.Print;
end;
```

When the Print button is pressed, this procedure will print an exact copy of the form as currently displayed.

Printer commands

The **Printer** object is used for giving commands directly to the printer. In order to use it, you must add Printers to the Uses statement. The Printer has a Canvas property, which works in the same way as for the form. The **TextOut** command prints a specific piece of text at a specified position on the screen. The various **Font** properties determine the appearance of the text. **NewPage** starts a new page. Before printing to the canvas, initialise the printer with **BeginDoc**; **EndDoc** tells the printer that printing has finished.

The following program demonstrates the use of these commands.

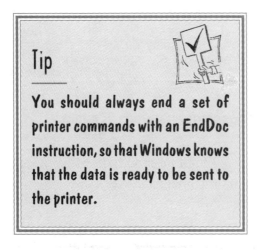

Tip

You should always end a set of printer commands with an EndDoc instruction, so that Windows knows that the data is ready to be sent to the printer.

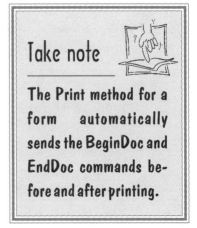

Take note

The Print method for a form automatically sends the BeginDoc and EndDoc commands before and after printing.

Report printing

```
procedure TReportForm.MenuFilePrintClick
                                (Sender: TObject);
var
    TitleMsg: string;
    TitleWidth: Integer;
    X, Y: Integer;
begin
    TitleMsg := 'Annual Report';
    with Printer do
        {All properties assumed to apply to Printer}
        begin
            BeginDoc;     {Initialise printer}
            Canvas.Font.Size := 24;
            Canvas.Font.Style := [fsBold];

            {Calculate width of text at 24 point bold}
            TitleWidth := Printer.Canvas.TextWidth(TitleMsg);

            {Set print position and print}
            X := (PageWidth - TitleWidth) div 2;
            Y := PageHeight div 3;
            Canvas.TextOut(X, Y, TitleMsg);
            NewPage;        {Force form feed}

            {Print other text and then send to printer}
            PrintContents; {Call procedure to print contents page}
            EndDoc;     {Send to printer}
        end;

    {Print remainder of report direct from screen displays}
    MainReportForm.Print;     {Print second page}
    SummaryForm.Print;        {Print final page}
end;
```

Exercises

1 Add a bitmap to the Contacts program's front screen.

2 Add a File | Print command to the Contacts program's font screen, so that the full details, including call notes, can be printed.

For solutions to these exercises, see page 196.

11 Solutions to exercises

1   Overview (p16)

1   Click on the Start button, Programs, the Borland Delphi 3 folder and the Delphi 3 application icon.

The main window (including the title bar, menu bar, speedbar and component palette) Object Inspector, Form1 and part of code window should be visible.

2   Close the Object Inspector window by double-clicking on the Control-menu box or the Close button; re-open by selecting from the View menu. Hide Form1 and the code window by clicking on their Minimise buttons; restore by clicking on the same buttons. Move windows by dragging the title bar; resize by dragging edges or corners. Maximise by clicking on the Maximise button.

3   Click on the Help menu, then Keyword Search (or select Contents and click on the Index tab). In the first box, type 'obj', then double-click on 'Object Inspector' and, in the Topics Found window, double-click on 'About the Object Inspector'.

4   Click on the Minimise button in the main window.

Click on Delphi 3 in the taskbar.

5   Click on File in the main window menu bar and then on Exit.

2   Forms (p30)

(Note that the dimensions of these forms do not have to be exactly as given below - the suggested values are for a higer-resolution screen.)

1   In Windows Explorer, click on (C:) and then on File|New|Folder. Enter 'Contacts' as the name.

2   Change the properties for Form1 as follows:

Name:	MainForm
Caption:	Contacts Manager
BorderStyle:	bsSingle
biMinimize:	True (default)
biMaximize:	False
Left, Top :	150 x 100
Width x Height :	500 x 400

Save with File|Save As in MainUnit.pas

3   Use File|New Form to add a form. Change the properties as follows:

Name:	DetailsForm
Caption:	Contact Details
BorderStyle:	bsSingle
biMinimize:	True (default)
biMaximize:	False
Left, Top:	280, 80
Width x Height:	400 x 350

Save with File|Save As, naming it DetlUnit.pas (or similar).

2 Forms (continued)

4 Use File|New Form to add a form. Change the properties as follows:

Name:	CallForm
Caption:	Call Details
BorderStyle:	bsSizeable (default)
bsMinimize:	True (default)
bsMaximize:	True (default)
Left, Top:	80, 240
Width x Height:	440 x 300

Save with File|Save As, naming the file CallUnit.pas (or similar).

5 Use File|Save Project As.

6 Press **[F9]** to run the application.The first window should be displayed. Click on the Close box to close it down. Press **[Ctrl-S]** to resave the project.

3 Components (p54)

1 Component properties are as follows:

Labels

Name:	LabelTitle	LabelVersion
Caption:	Contacts Manager	Version 1.0
AutoSize:	False	False
Alignment:	taCenter	taCenter
Font:	14 point, bold	10 point, bold
Left, Top:	152, 32	152, 64
Width x Height:	170 x 24	170 x 24

Command buttons

Name:	ButtonDetails	ButtonCalls
Caption:	Contact &Details	&Calls
Default:	True	False (default)
Cancel:	False (default)	False (default)
Left, Top:	56 x 304	200, 304
Width x Height:	97 x 25	97 x 25

Name:	ButtonExit
Caption:	E&xit
Default:	False (default)
Cancel:	True
Left, Top:	344, 304
Width x Height:	97 x 25

2 Use File|New Form to add a new form. Change the properties as follows:

Name:	PasswordForm
Caption:	Password
BorderStyle:	bsDialog

biSystemMenu:	False	
biMinimize:	False	
biMaximize:	False	
Left, Top:	269, 159	
Width x Height:	276 x 167	

Add the following components:

Label

Name:	LabelEnter
Caption:	Enter your &password:
FocusControl:	EditPassword
Font:	10 point
Left, Top:	72, 24
Width x Height:	125 x 16

Text box

Name:	EditPassword
Text:	(blank)
Font:	10 point
PasswordChar:	*
Left, Top:	72, 48
Width x Height:	129 x 24

Command buttons

Name:	ButtonOK	ButtonCancel
Caption:	&OK	&Cancel
Default:	True	False
Cancel:	False	True
Left, Top:	40, 96	160, 96
Width x Height:	75 x 25	75 x 25

Save the form as PwdUnit.pas (or similar) in the Contacts directory.

3   Component properties are as follows:

Labels (form)

Name:	LabelName	LabelCompany
Caption:	Name:	Company:
Alignment:	taRightJustify	taRightJustify
Font:	10 point	10 point
Left, Top:	8, 16	194, 16
Width x Height:	49 x 16	71 x 16

Edit boxes (form)

Name:	EditName	EditCompany
Font:	10 point	10 point
Text:	(blank)	(blank)
Left, Top:	64, 16	264, 16
Width x Height:	113 x 24	113 x 24

3 Controls (continued)

Group boxes

Name:	AddressFrame	ContactFrame
Caption:	Address details	Contact Numbers
Left, Top:	8, 48	200, 48
Width x Height	177 x 121	177 x 121

Labels (Address details)

Name:	LabelFullName	LabelAddress
Caption:	&Full Name:	&Address:
Alignment:	taRightJustify	taRightJustify
Focus Control:	EditFullName	MemoAddress
Left, Top:	8, 28	8, 52
Width x Height:	49 x 13	49 x 13

Text boxes (Address details)

Type:	*Editbox*	*Memo*
Name:	EditFullName	MemoAddress
Text:	(blank)	
Left, Top:	64, 24	64, 48
Width x Height:	105 x 21	105 x 65

Labels (Contact numbers)

Name:	LabelWork	LabelMobile
Caption:	&Work:	&Mobile:
Alignment::	taRightJustify	taRightJustify
FocusControl:	EditWork	EditMobile
Left, Top:	8, 28	8, 52
Width x Height:	42 x 13	42 x 13

Name:	LabelFax	LabelEMail
Caption:	Fa&x:	&E-Mail:
Alignment::	taRightJustify	taRightJustify
FocusControl:	EditFax	EditEMail
Left, Top:	8, 76	8, 100
Width x Height:	42 x 13	42 x 13

Radio group

Name:	RadioCType
Caption:	Contact type
Items:	&Sales; Su&pport; &Consultancy
ItemIndex:	0
Left, Top:	8, 184
Width x Height	113 x 89

Panel

Name:	PanelUpdates
Caption:	(blank)
Left, Top:	136, 192
Width x Height:	105 x 81

3   Controls (continued)

Labels (panel)

Name:	LabelBy	LabelOn
Caption:	&Updated by	o&n
FocusControl:	EditBy	EditOn
Left, Top:	8, 20	16, 52
Width x Height:	55 x 13	12 x 13

Edit boxes (panel)

Name:	EditBy	EditOn
Text:	(blank)	(blank)
Left, Top:	72, 16	40, 48
Width x Height:	25 x 21	57 x 21

Label (form)

Name:	LabelNotes
Caption:	&Notes
FocusControl:	MemoNotes
Left, Top:	256, 184
Width x Height:	28 x 13

Memo (form)

Name:	MemoNotes
Left, Top:	256, 200
Width x Height:	121 x 73

Command buttons (form)

Name:	ButtonOK	ButtonCancel
Caption:	&OK	&Cancel
Default:	True	False
Cancel:	False	True
Left, Top:	88, 288	216, 288
Width x Height:	75 x 25	75 x 25

4   Use **[Ctrl-C]** to copy LabelName, EditName, LabelAddress and EditAddress from DetailsForm and **[Ctrl-V]** to paste them into CallsForm.

The other components' properties are as follows:

Labels

Name:	LabelDate	LabelTime
Caption:	&Date	&Time:
FocusControl:	EditDate	EditTime
Left, Top:	24, 52	224, 52

Edit boxes

Name:	EditDate	EditTime
Text:	(blank)	(blank)
Left, Top:	64, 48	264, 48
Width x Height:	121 x 21	121 x 21

3 Controls (continued)

Memo

Name:	MemoCallnote
ScrollBars:	ssVertical
Left, Top:	16, 80
Width x Height:	400, 153

Command buttons

Name:	ButtonNext
Caption:	&Next
Left, Top:	32, 240
Width x Height:	75, 25

Copy the OK and Cancel buttons from Details, using **[Ctrl-C]** and **[Ctrl-V]**.

5 Save using File | Save All. Run the program by pressing **[F9]**. You can click on any of the three command buttons but they will have no effect as yet.

Close the program with Run | Program Reset or by clicking on the Close box.

4 Coding events (p80)

(To save space, most blank lines have been removed from program listings.)

1 Display MainForm, double-click on the Contact Details button and enter the following procedure in the Code window:

```
procedure TMainForm.ButtonDetailsClick(Sender: TObject);
begin
  DetailsForm.Show;
end
```

(Note that the first two lines and last line are provided for you.)

2 Double-click on the Calls button and enter the following procedure:

```
procedure TMainForm.ButtonCallsClick(Sender: TObject);
begin
  CallsForm.Show
end;
```

3 Double-click on the Exit button and enter the following procedure:

```
procedure TMainForm.ButtonExitClick(Sender: TObject);
begin
  Mainform.Close;
end;
```

4 Double-click on a blank area of the form and enter the following procedure:

```
procedure TMainForm.FormCreate(Sender: TObject);
begin
  MainForm.Left := (Screen.Width - MainForm.Width) div 2;
  MainForm.Top := (Screen.Height - MainForm.Height) div 2;
end;
```

4   Coding events (continued)

5   Display the Details form and add the following components:

> *Label*
> Name: LabelOrgType
> Caption: &Org Type
> FocusControl: ComboOrgType
> Left, Top: 256, 184
> Width x Height: 448 x 13
>
> *Combo box*
> Name: ComboOrgType
> Text: (blank)
> Style: csDropDownList
> Sorted: True
> Left, Top: 256, 200
> Width x Height: 121 x 21

Double-click on the Items property and list the organisation types using the string list editor.

6   Double-click on the OK button and enter the following procedure:

```
procedure TDetailsForm.ButtonOKClick(Sender: TObject);
begin
  DetailsForm.Close;
end;
```

Double-click on the Cancel button and enter the following procedure:

```
procedure TDetailsForm.ButtonCancelClick(Sender: TObject);
begin
  DetailsForm.Close;
end;
```

7   Display the Calls form and click on the Events tab in the Object Inspector. Double-click to the right of OnResize and enter the following procedure:

```
procedure TCallsForm.FormResize(Sender: TObject);
begin
  MemoCallnote.Height := CallsForm.ClientHeight - MemoCallnote.Top - 40;
  MemoCallnote.Width := CallsForm.ClientWidth - 31;
  ButtonOK.Left := (CallsForm.ClientWidth - ButtonOK.Width) div 2;
  ButtonCancel.Left := MemoCallnote.Left + MemoCallnote.Width
    - ButtonCancel.Width - 16;
  ButtonNext.Top := CallsForm.ClientHeight - ButtonNext.Height - 8;
  ButtonOK.Top := ButtonNext.Top;
  ButtonCancel.Top := ButtonNext.Top;
end;
```

4 Coding events (continued)

8 Double-click on the OK button and enter the following procedure:

```
procedure TCallsForm.ButtonOKClick(Sender: TObject);
begin
  CallsForm.Close;
end;
```

Double-click on the Cancel button and enter the following procedure:

```
procedure TCallsForm.ButtonCancelClick(Sender: TObject);
begin
  CallsForm.Close;
end;
```

5 Variables (p104)

1 Set up the form and add the following procedures:

```
const
  CmPerInch = 2.54;
  KgPerLb = 0.453;
  LitresPerPint = 0.568;

procedure TConvForm.ButtonInchCmClick(Sender: TObject);
var
  Inches, Cm: Single;
  SCm: string;
begin
  Inches := StrToFloat(EditEntry.Text);
  Cm := Inches * CmPerInch;
  Str(Cm:12:2, SCm);
  EditResult.Text := Trim(SCm);
  LabelEntry.Caption := 'Inches';
  LabelResult.Caption := 'cm';
end;

procedure TConvForm.ButtonCmInchClick(Sender: TObject);
var
  Inches, Cm: Single;
  SInches: string;
begin
  Cm := StrToFloat(EditEntry.Text);
  Inches := Cm / CmPerInch;
  Str(Inches:12:2, SInches);
  EditResult.Text := Trim(SInches);
  LabelEntry.Caption := 'cm';
  LabelResult.Caption := 'Inches';
end;
```

Add similar procedures for the other four buttons

```
procedure TConvForm.EditEntryChange(Sender: TObject);
begin
  LabelEntry.Caption := 'Entry:';
  LabelResult.Caption := 'Result:';
  EditResult.Text := '';
end;

procedure TConvForm.ButtonExitClick(Sender: TObject);
begin
  ConvForm.Close;
end;
```

The Result box's Enabled property should be False. None of the buttons has a Default property set to True.

2   The procedure is as follows:

```
procedure TDetailsForm.ComboOrgTypeClick(Sender: TObject);
var
  Dept: array [0..5] of string;
  CurrentOrg: Integer;
  CurrentDept: string;
begin
  Dept[0] := 'Commercial';  {Company}
  Dept[1] := 'Commercial';  {Consultant}
  Dept[2] := 'Local Govt';  {Council}
  Dept[3] := 'Local Govt';  {Educational}
  Dept[4] := 'Personal';    {Other}
  Dept[5] := 'Personal';    {Private}
  CurrentOrg := ComboOrgType.ItemIndex;
  CurrentDept := Dept[CurrentOrg];
  LabelDept.Caption := 'Dept:  ' + CurrentDept;
end;
```

3   The following program uses two edit boxes for entering the dates (EditDate1 and EditDate2) and two for showing the results (EditDays and EditWeeks). The calculation is initiated by clicking on a button (ButtonCalculate).

```
procedure TDatesForm.ButtonCalculateClick(Sender: TObject);
var
  Days1, Days2: TDateTime;
  NumWeeks, NumDays: Integer;
begin
  Days1 := StrToDateTime(EditDate1.Text);
  Days2 := StrToDateTime(EditDate2.Text);
  NumWeeks := Trunc(Days2 - Days1) div 7;
  NumDays := Trunc(Days2 - Days1) mod 7;
  EditWeeks.Text := IntToStr(NumWeeks);
  EditDays.Text := IntToStr(NumDays);
end;
```

6 Basic instructions (p132)

1 The procedure is as follows:

```
procedure DateCalc(DateIn: string; Extra: Integer; var DateOut: string);
var
  Period: Byte;
  DateInDT, DateOutDT: TDateTime;
  DayIn, MonthIn, YearIn: Word;
  MonthOut, YearOut: Word;
begin
  {Get date units: 0 Days, 1 Weeks, 2 Months, 3 Years}
  Period := DateForm.RadioPeriod.ItemIndex;
  {Unpack incoming date}
  DateInDT := StrToDateTime(DateIn);
  DecodeDate(DateInDT, YearIn, MonthIn, DayIn);

  {Calculate new date}
  case Period of
  0 {Days}   : DateOutDT := DateInDT + Extra;
  1 {Weeks}  : DateOutDT := DateInDT + Extra * 7;
  2 {Months} : begin
            MonthOut := ((MonthIn + Extra - 1) mod 12) + 1;
            YearOut := YearIn + ((MonthIn + Extra - 1) div 12);
            DateOutDT := EncodeDate(YearOut, MonthOut, DayIn);
        end;
  3 {Years}  : begin
            YearOut := YearIn + Extra;
            DateOutDT := EncodeDate(YearOut, MonthIn, DayIn);
        end;
  else
    DateOutDT := DateInDT;
  end;
  DateOut := FormatDateTime('dd/mm/yyyy', DateOutDT);
end;
```

2 The function is as follows:

```
function PasswordOK(Password: string): Boolean;
var
  CorrectPassword: string;
begin
  {Add code here to read correct password from file
   - assuming correct password is 'pass'}
  CorrectPassword := 'pass';
  if Password = CorrectPassword then
    PasswordOK := True
  else
    PasswordOK := False;
end;
```

6   Basic instructions (continued)

3   The three controls at the top of the window have the following properties:

Combo box

Name:	ComboMonth
Sorted:	False
Style:	csDropDownList
Items:	January, February etc.

Edit box

Name:	EditYear
Text:	(blank)

Command button

Name:	ButtonRedisplay
Caption:	&Redisplay
Default:	True

Properties for the grid are given on page 127.

The Implementation section of the program is as follows:

```
implementation

{$R *.DFM}

var
  Weekdays: array [1..7] of string;

procedure FillDays(CalMonth, CalYear: Integer);
var
  Row, Col: Integer;
  DayNum: Integer;
  FirstDay, LastDay: TDateTime;
  FirstWeekDay, DaysNotUsed: Byte;
  NextYear, NextMonth: Word;
  DaysInMonth: Byte;
begin
  {Find day of week for first day (Sunday = 1)
   - hence number of days not used in Week 1}
  FirstDay := EncodeDate(CalYear, CalMonth, 1);
  FirstWeekDay := DayOfWeek(FirstDay) - 1;
  if FirstWeekDay = 0 then FirstWeekDay := 7; {move Sunday}
  DaysNotUsed := FirstWeekDay - 1;

  {Find number of days in month}
  NextYear := CalYear;
  NextMonth := CalMonth + 1;
  if NextMonth = 13 then
    begin
      NextMonth := 1;
      NextYear := CalYear + 1;
    end;
```

```
    LastDay := EncodeDate(NextYear, NextMonth, 1) - 1;
    DaysInMonth := Round(LastDay - FirstDay) + 1;

    {Fill in day numbers}
    DayNum := 1;
    for Col := 1 to 11 do
      if Col in [1, 3, 5, 7, 9, 11] then
        for Row := 0 to 6 do
          begin
            if ((Col = 1) and (Row < DaysNotUsed))
              or (DayNum > DaysInMonth) then
                {Before first day of month or after last day}
                CalendarForm.GridDay.Cells[Col, Row] := ''
            else
              {Valid day of month}
              begin
                CalendarForm.GridDay.Cells[Col, Row] := IntToStr(DayNum);
                DayNum := DayNum + 1;
              end;
          end;
end;

procedure TCalendarForm.FormCreate(Sender: TObject);
var
  Row, Col: Integer;
  CurrentYear, CurrentMonth, CurrentDay: Word;
begin
  {Set up array of weekdays}
  Weekdays[1] := 'Monday';
  Weekdays[2] := 'Tuesday';
  Weekdays[3] := 'Wednesday';
  Weekdays[4] := 'Thursday';
  Weekdays[5] := 'Friday';
  Weekdays[6] := 'Saturday';
  Weekdays[7] := 'Sunday';
  {Fill in day names}
  for Row := 0 to 6 do
    GridDay.Cells[0, Row] := Weekdays[Row + 1];
  {Reduce size of alternate cells}
  for Col := 1 to 11 do
    if Col in [1, 3, 5, 7, 9, 11] then
      GridDay.ColWidths[Col] := 16;
  {Set initial values of month and year and fill in days}
  DecodeDate(Date, CurrentYear, CurrentMonth, CurrentDay);
  ComboMonth.ItemIndex := CurrentMonth - 1;
  EditYear.Text := IntToStr(CurrentYear);
  FillDays(CurrentMonth, CurrentYear);
end;
```

189

```
procedure TCalendarForm.GridDaySelectCell(Sender: TObject; Col,
  Row: Integer; var CanSelect: Boolean);
begin
  {Enable even-numbered columns only}
  GridDay.Options :=
[goFixedVertLine,goFixedHorzLine,goVertLine,goHorzLine,goRangeSelect];
  if Col in [2, 4, 6, 8, 10, 12] then
    if GridDay.Cells[Col - 1, Row] > '0' then
      {Enable only if day label shown to left}
      GridDay.Options :=
[goFixedVertLine,goFixedHorzLine,goVertLine,goHorzLine,goRangeSelect,goEditing];
  end;

procedure TCalendarForm.ComboMonthClick(Sender: TObject);
begin
  ButtonRedisplayClick(Sender);
end;

procedure TCalendarForm.EditYearExit(Sender: TObject);
begin
  ButtonRedisplayClick(Sender);
end;

procedure TCalendarForm.ButtonRedisplayClick(Sender: TObject);
var
  CurrentYear, CurrentMonth: Word;
begin
  CurrentMonth := ComboMonth.ItemIndex + 1;
  CurrentYear := StrToInt(EditYear.Text);
  FillDays(CurrentMonth, CurrentYear);
end;

end.
```

7   Error handling (p140)

1   Use the Project Manager to display the DetlUnit code window. Click on the blue dot to the left of the Begin line of TDetailsForm.ComboOrgTypeClick, so that the line is highlighted in red.

Press **[F9]** to run the program, click on Contact Details and the Org Type drop-down box. Click on an item in the list to break into the program.

Press **[F7]** to single-step through the program. Click on CurrentOrg and press **[Ctrl-F5]** and **[Enter]**. Highlight LabelDept.Caption, press **[Ctrl-C]**, **[Ctrl-F5]**, **[Ctrl-V]** and **[Enter]**. Click on the the Watch List, press the right-hand mouse button and select Stay on Top.

Single-step with **[F8]** and watch the Watch List window.

7 Error handling (continued)

2 Amend the procedure as follows:

```
procedure TCalendarForm.ButtonRedisplayClick(Sender: TObject);
var
  CurrentYear, CurrentMonth, CurrentDay: Word;
begin
  CurrentMonth := ComboMonth.ItemIndex + 1;
  try
    CurrentYear := StrToInt(EditYear.Text);
  except
    begin
      DecodeDate(Date, CurrentYear, CurrentMonth, CurrentDay);
      EditYear.Text := IntToStr(CurrentYear);
      CurrentYear := StrToInt(EditYear.Text);
    end;
  end;
  FillDays(CurrentMonth, CurrentYear);
end;
```

8 Menus (p150)

1 The menus and procedures are as follows:

```
procedure TMainForm.MenuFileExitClick
                            (Sender: TObject);
begin
  ButtonExitClick(Sender);
end;
```

```
procedure TMainForm.MenuWindowContactsClick
                            (Sender: TObject);
begin
  ButtonDetailsClick(Sender);
end;
```

```
procedure TMainForm.MenuWindowCallsClick(Sender: TObject);
begin
  ButtonCallsClick(Sender);
end;

procedure TMainForm.MenuWindowCloseAllClick(Sender: TObject);
begin
  {Accept changes (i.e. click OK), close windows}
  DetailsForm.ButtonOKClick(Sender);
  CallsForm.ButtonOKClick(Sender);
end;

procedure TMainForm.MenuHelpAboutClick(Sender: TObject);
var
  VersionString, AboutString: string;
```

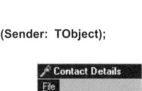

```
begin
  VersionString := 'Version ' + IntToStr(VersionNo)
              + '.' + IntToStr(SubVersion);
  AboutString := 'Contacts Manager ' + VersionString;
  MessageDlg(AboutString, mtInformation, [mbOK], 0);
end;
```

2   The menus and procedures are as follows:

```
procedure TDetailsForm.MenuFileAbandonClick(Sender: TObject);
begin
  ButtonCancelClick(Sender);
end;

procedure TDetailsForm.MenuFileExitClick
                    (Sender: TObject);
begin
  ButtonOKClick(Sender);
end;
```

3   Add Clipbrd to the Uses statement. The menus and procedures are as follows:

```
procedure TCallsForm.MenuFileAbandonClick(Sender: TObject);
begin
  ButtonCancelClick(Sender);
end;

procedure TCallsForm.MenuFileExitClick
                    (Sender: TObject);
begin
  ButtonCancelClick(Sender);
end;

procedure TCallsForm.MenuEditCutClick
                    (Sender: TObject);
begin
  Clipboard.Clear;
  Clipboard.AsText := MemoCallnote.SelText;
  MemoCallnote.SelText := '';
end;
```

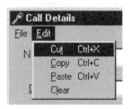

```
procedure TCallsForm.MenuEditCopyClick(Sender: TObject);
begin
  Clipboard.Clear;
  Clipboard.AsText := MemoCallnote.SelText;
end;

procedure TCallsForm.MenuEditPasteClick(Sender: TObject);
begin
  MemoCallnote.SelText := Clipboard.AsText;
end;
```

8 Menus (continued)

```
procedure  TCallsForm.MenuEditClearClick(Sender: TObject);
var
  MsgButton: Integer;
begin
  MsgButton := MessageDlg('Call text will be deleted! Continue?', mtWarning,
[mbYes, mbNo], 0);
  if MsgButton = mrYes then
    MemoCallnote.Text := '';
end;
```

9 Files (p168)

1   Add the following components:

> *Combo box*
> Name: ComboBoxCList
> Style: csDropdown
> Text: (blank)
>
> *Command button*
> Name: ButtonAddContact
> Caption: Add Contact

Add the following procedure:

```
procedure  TMainForm.ButtonAddContactClick(Sender: TObject);
begin
  ComboBoxCList.Items.Add(ComboBoxCList.Text);
end;
```

2.   Add a SaveDialog component to MainForm and add the following procedure. (Error-handling has been omitted to save space.)

```
procedure  TMainForm.MenuFileSaveClick(Sender: TObject);
var
  ConFile: textfile;
  FName: string;
  i: Integer;
const
  CR = Chr(13) + Chr(10);
begin
  SaveDialog1.Filter := 'Contact files (*.con)|*.con';
  SaveDialog1.Execute;
  FName := SaveDialog1.FileName;
  if UpperCase(Copy(FName, Length(FName) - 3, 4)) <> '.CON' then
    FName := FName + '.CON';
  AssignFile(ConFile, FName);
  Rewrite(ConFile);
```

193

9 Files (continued)

```
      for i := 0 to ComboBoxCList.Items.Count - 1 do
        begin
          ComboBoxCList.ItemIndex := i;
            Write(ConFile, ComboBoxCList.Text, CR);
        end;
      CloseFile(ConFile);
    end;
```

3   Add a OpenDialog component to MainForm and add the following procedure:

procedure TMainForm.MenuFileOpenClick(Sender: TObject);
```
    var
      ConFile: textfile;
      ContactName: string;
    begin
      OpenDialog1.Filter := 'Contact files (*.con)|*.con';
      OpenDialog1.Execute;
      LabelFName.Caption := OpenDialog1.FileName;
      AssignFile(ConFile, OpenDialog1.FileName);
      Reset(ConFile);
      while not eof(ConFile) do
        begin
          ReadLn(ConFile, ContactName);
           ComboBoxCList.Items.Add(ContactName);
        end;
      CloseFile(ConFile);
    end;
```

4   Add the following procedures to CallsForm:

procedure TCallsForm.MenuFileSaveClick(Sender: TObject);
```
    var
      ConFile: textfile;
      FName: string;
    const
      CR = Chr(13) + Chr(10);
    begin
      FName := 'CON' + Trim(IntToStr(MainForm.ComboBoxCList.ItemIndex + 1))
                                                                 + '.TXT';
      AssignFile(ConFile, FName);
      Rewrite(ConFile);
      Write(ConFile, EditDate.Text, CR, EditTime.Text, CR, MemoCallnote.Text);
      CloseFile(ConFile);
    end;
```

5   Add the following procedures to CallsForm:

procedure TCallsForm.FormActivate(Sender: TObject);
```
    var
      ConFile: textfile;
      FName, InputText: string;
```

```
begin
  FName := 'CON' + Trim(IntToStr(MainForm.ComboBoxCList.ItemIndex + 1))
+ '.TXT';
  try
    AssignFile(ConFile, FName);
    Reset(ConFile);
    ReadLn(ConFile, InputText);
    EditDate.Text := InputText;
    ReadLn(ConFile, InputText);
    EditTime.Text := InputText;
    ReadLn(ConFile, InputText);
    MemoCallnote.Text := InputText;
    CloseFile(ConFile);
  except
    on EInOutError do;
  end;
end;
```

6 Add the following declaration at the top of the DetailsForm Implementation section:

```
type
  DetRecType =
    record
      ContactName: string[25];
      Company: string[30];
      ContactType: Integer;
      {add fields for other screen entries}
    end;
  DetFileType = file of DetRecType;
```

Add the following procedure to DetailsForm:

```
procedure  TDetailsForm.MenuFileSaveClick(Sender:  TObject);
var
  DetFile: DetFileType;
  DetRec: DetRecType;
  RecNo: Integer;
begin
  AssignFile(DetFile, MainForm.LabelFName.Caption);
  Reset(DetFile);
  RecNo := MainForm.ComboBoxCList.ItemIndex + 1;
  with DetRec do
    begin
      ContactName := EditName.Text;
      Company := EditCompany.Text;
      ContactType := RadioCType.ItemIndex;
    end;
```

9   Files (continued)

```
      Seek(DetFile, RecNo);
      Write(DetFile, DetRec);
      CloseFile(DetFile);
    end;
```

7.   Add the following procedure to DetailsForm:

```
procedure TDetailsForm.FormActivate(Sender: TObject);
var
  DetFile: DetFileType;
  DetRec: DetRecType;
  RecNo: Integer;
begin
  AssignFile(DetFile, MainForm.LabelFName.Caption);
  Reset(DetFile);
  RecNo := MainForm.ComboBoxCList.ItemIndex + 1;
  try
    Seek(DetFile, RecNo);
    Read(DetFile, DetRec);
    with DetRec do
      begin
        EditName.Text := ContactName;
        EditCompany.Text := Company;
        RadioCType.ItemIndex := ContactType;
      end;
  except
    on EInOutError do;
  end;
  CloseFile(DetFile);
end;
```

10   Graphics (p176)

1   Add an image control to MainForm. Use its Picture property to select a bitmap.

2   Add a Print option to the File menu and enter the following procedure:

```
procedure TMainForm.MenuFilePrintClick(Sender: TObject);
begin
    DetailsForm.Print;      {Print details form}
    CallsForm.Print;        {Print calls form}
end;
```

You can now extend the Contacts program to make it a useful application.

Index

M 212337

SE- 18% x 1 = 11.79